HOW TO AVOID BEING SCAMMED

A Comprehensive Guide to Fraud
Prevention and Recovery

Jacalina Gonzaga

A&A Publishers (Calgary)

CONTENTS

Title Page

Prologue

Introduction 1

Chapter 1 Understanding Scams 20

Chapter 2 Recognizing Red Flags 56

Chapter 3 Real-Life Examples 71

Chapter 4 Protecting Yourself Online 85

Chapter 5 Dealing with Scammers 99

Chapter 6 Preventative Measures 112

Chapter 7 Scams Targeting Specific Groups 128

Chapter 8 International Scams 143

Chapter 9 Resources and Help 158

Chapter 10 Technological Advances and Scams 169

Chapter 11 Psychological Resilience 182

Chapter 12 Educating the Next Generation 196

Chapter 13 Scam Trends and Future Predictions 208

Afterword 227

PROLOGUE

In an age where technology permeates every aspect of our lives, the digital world offers boundless opportunities and conveniences. From online banking to social media, from e-commerce to virtual classrooms, we live in an interconnected landscape that was unimaginable just a few decades ago. However, with these advancements comes an inherent risk: the rise of sophisticated scams and frauds that prey on our trust and vulnerability.

Imagine receiving an urgent email from what appears to be your bank, warning you of unauthorized access to your account and urging you to verify your details immediately. Or perhaps you stumble upon an incredible deal online for a high-end smartphone at a fraction of its retail price. Maybe a charming individual on a dating site confides in you, sharing their woes and eventually asking for financial assistance. These scenarios are not mere hypotheticals; they are real-life instances of scams that have ensnared countless victims, causing emotional and financial devastation.

This book, "How to Avoid Being Scammed: A Comprehensive Guide to Fraud Prevention and Recovery," is born out of the necessity to arm individuals with the knowledge and tools to navigate this treacherous landscape. It is a call to vigilance, a roadmap to safeguarding your assets, and a beacon of hope for those who have already fallen victim to deceit.

Our journey begins with an exploration of the various types of scams, delving into their mechanics and the psychology that makes them so effective. We will uncover the tactics scammers use to manipulate their targets, from phishing emails to deepfake technology, and how they exploit emerging trends like cryptocurrencies and the Internet of Things (IoT).

Education is our strongest defense. By understanding the red flags and implementing robust preventative measures, we can reduce the risk of falling prey to these nefarious schemes. Through interactive elements such as quizzes, scenario analyses, and practical exercises, this book will transform you from a potential victim into a vigilant defender of your personal and financial security.

But what if you have already been scammed? This guide extends beyond prevention to offer a lifeline for recovery. We provide detailed strategies for dealing with scammers, reporting fraud, seeking legal recourse, and rebuilding your life after an incident. Emotional resilience is as important as financial recovery, and we delve into coping strategies, support networks, and counseling services to help you heal and emerge stronger.

As we look to the future, we must remain adaptive and proactive. The landscape of scams is ever-evolving, with new threats on the horizon. This book will equip you with the foresight to anticipate these changes, drawing on expert insights and the latest research in cybersecurity.

Ultimately, "How to Avoid Being Scammed" is more than a guide; it is a testament to the power of knowledge and the resilience of the human spirit. Whether you are reading this book to protect yourself, educate others, or recover from a past experience, know that you are not alone. Together, we can create a safer, more informed world, where trust is not a vulnerability but a strength.

Welcome to your comprehensive journey into fraud prevention and recovery. Let us begin this vital quest for awareness, protection, and empowerment.

INTRODUCTION

Purpose of the Book

The purpose of this book is to empower individuals with the knowledge and tools necessary to recognize, avoid, and combat scams. In an increasingly digital world, scams have become more sophisticated and pervasive, posing significant risks to personal security, financial stability, and overall well-being. This book aims to provide comprehensive guidance on how to navigate this complex landscape, ensuring readers are equipped to protect themselves and their loved ones from fraudulent activities.

Understanding the Need for Awareness

Scams are not a new phenomenon; they have existed for centuries in various forms. However, the advent of the internet and modern communication technologies has dramatically increased the scope and scale of scams. Today, scammers can reach millions of potential victims globally with minimal effort. According to a report by the Federal Trade Commission (FTC), consumers reported losing more than $3.3 billion to fraud in 2020, a significant increase from previous years. These figures underscore the urgent need for heightened awareness and proactive measures.

Who Can Benefit from This Book?

This book is designed for a broad audience, including:

- **Individuals of All Ages**: From teenagers to senior

citizens, everyone can benefit from understanding how scams operate and how to avoid them.

- **Business Owners and Professionals**: Businesses are often targeted by scams, and professional individuals need to be aware of potential threats to protect their enterprises and careers.

- **Educators and Community Leaders**: Those in positions of influence can use the knowledge gained from this book to educate others and foster a more informed community.

- **Parents and Guardians**: Protecting children and teenagers from online scams and teaching them safe internet practices is crucial in today's digital age.

Goals and Objectives

The primary goals and objectives of this book are to:

1. **Educate Readers About Various Types of Scams**: Provide detailed explanations of different scam tactics, including online scams, phone scams, and in-person scams.

2. **Enhance Awareness of Red Flags**: Help readers identify common warning signs of scams, such as offers that are too good to be true, high-pressure tactics, and requests for unusual payment methods.

3. **Offer Practical Advice and Strategies**: Equip readers with actionable steps to protect themselves from scams, including safe internet practices, financial safeguards, and reporting mechanisms.

4. **Provide Real-Life Examples and Case Studies**: Illustrate how scams operate through detailed case studies and examples, helping readers understand the

real-world impact of scams and how to avoid falling victim.

5. **Promote Psychological Resilience and Support**: Address the emotional and psychological aspects of dealing with scams, offering guidance on building resilience and accessing support networks.

6. **Foster a Culture of Vigilance and Proactivity**: Encourage readers to stay informed about new and emerging scams, share knowledge with others, and take proactive measures to safeguard their personal and financial security.

Scope of the Book

This book covers a wide range of topics related to scams and fraud prevention. Each chapter is designed to build on the previous ones, creating a comprehensive and cohesive guide. The scope includes:

- **Types of Scams**: Detailed descriptions of various scams, including online scams (phishing, fake websites), phone scams (robocalls, IRS impersonations), and in-person scams (fake charities, lottery scams).

- **Recognizing Red Flags**: Identification of common scam indicators and warning signs that can help readers spot fraudulent activities early.

- **Protecting Yourself Online**: Guidelines for safe internet practices, including secure browsing, social media awareness, and secure online transactions.

- **Dealing with Scammers**: Steps to take if targeted by a scam, including reporting mechanisms and legal recourse.

- **Preventative Measures**: Strategies for educating oneself and others, financial safeguards, and utilizing technology tools to enhance security.

- **Scams Targeting Specific Groups**: Focused advice for protecting vulnerable populations, businesses, and students from targeted scams.

- **International Scams**: Understanding global scam trends and how to protect oneself while traveling or dealing with international transactions.

- **Technological Advances and Scams**: Exploration of how modern technologies, such as artificial intelligence and cryptocurrency, are used in scams and how to stay ahead of these evolving threats.

- **Psychological Resilience**: Techniques for building mental fortitude, dealing with the emotional impact of scams, and finding support.

- **Educating the Next Generation**: Tips for teaching children and teenagers about scams and digital literacy.

- **Future Predictions**: Insights into emerging scam trends and expert predictions to help readers stay vigilant.

Importance of Proactive Measures

In the fight against scams, proactive measures are essential. This book emphasizes the importance of not only recognizing and avoiding scams but also taking proactive steps to prevent them. By educating themselves and others, individuals can create a ripple effect of awareness and protection within their communities. This proactive approach includes:

- **Staying Informed**: Keeping up to date with the latest scam tactics and trends through reliable sources such as government agencies, consumer protection organizations, and cybersecurity experts.

- **Sharing Knowledge**: Spreading awareness among family, friends, and colleagues to create a network of informed individuals who can collectively guard against scams.

- **Advocating for Stronger Protections**: Supporting policies and initiatives that enhance consumer protection and hold scammers accountable.

The purpose of this book is to arm readers with the knowledge and tools they need to stay safe in an increasingly complex and deceptive world. By understanding the nature of scams, recognizing red flags, and implementing practical safeguards, individuals can significantly reduce their risk of falling victim to fraud. Ultimately, this book aims to foster a culture of vigilance, proactivity, and resilience, empowering readers to protect themselves and contribute to a safer, more informed society.

Overview of Scams

Scams are fraudulent schemes designed to deceive individuals and extract money, personal information, or other valuable assets. While the tactics and methods of scammers have evolved over time, the fundamental principles remain the same: exploiting human vulnerabilities such as trust, greed, fear, and lack of awareness. This overview will explore the history of scams, the different types of scams prevalent today, and the impact these scams have on individuals and society.

Historical Context of Scams

Scams have a long and storied history, dating back to ancient times. One of the earliest recorded scams is the "pig in a poke" scheme from the Middle Ages, where a buyer would be sold a sack supposedly containing a valuable pig, only to find a less valuable animal or nothing at all inside. This scam gave rise to the cautionary phrase "don't buy a pig in a poke," highlighting the importance of verifying the value and authenticity of a purchase.

In the 19th century, the infamous "Spanish Prisoner" scam emerged, involving letters from supposed prisoners in Spain who promised large rewards in exchange for financial assistance. This scam is a precursor to modern email frauds, where scammers pose as individuals in distress to elicit money from unsuspecting victims.

With the advent of the 20th century and the rise of telecommunication, scams became more sophisticated. The infamous "Nigerian Prince" scam, also known as the 419 scam (named after the Nigerian criminal code for fraud), involves emails from a purportedly wealthy individual seeking help to transfer a large sum of money, promising a significant share in return. This scam persists today in various forms, exploiting people's willingness to trust and help others.

Types of Scams

Scams can be broadly categorized based on the medium through which they are perpetrated and the tactics used by scammers. Understanding these categories is crucial for recognizing and avoiding scams.

1. **Online Scams**
   - **Phishing**: Scammers send emails or messages that appear to be from legitimate sources, such as banks or popular websites, to trick individuals into revealing personal information, such as passwords or credit card numbers.

- **Fake Websites**: Scammers create counterfeit websites that mimic legitimate ones to deceive users into entering personal or financial information.

- **Social Media Scams**: Fraudulent schemes propagated through social media platforms, including fake giveaways, investment opportunities, and impersonation of trusted contacts.

2. **Phone Scams**
   - **Robocalls**: Automated calls that deliver prerecorded messages, often claiming to be from government agencies, financial institutions, or technical support services, urging recipients to take immediate action.

   - **Vishing (Voice Phishing)**: Scammers impersonate legitimate organizations over the phone, attempting to extract personal or financial information from the victim.

   - **Wangiri**: A type of phone scam where the victim receives a missed call from an international or premium-rate number, prompting them to return the call and incur high charges.

3. **In-Person Scams**
   - **Door-to-Door Scams**: Scammers pose as salespeople, utility workers, or charity representatives to gain access to homes and steal money or valuables.

   - **Lottery and Prize Scams**: Victims are informed that they have won a lottery or prize but must pay a fee or provide personal information to claim it.

- **Charity Scams**: Fraudsters solicit donations for fake charities, often exploiting natural disasters or crises to evoke sympathy and urgency.

4. **Financial Scams**
   - **Investment Scams**: Fraudulent investment opportunities promising high returns with little risk, such as Ponzi schemes or pyramid schemes.
   - **Credit Card Fraud**: Unauthorized use of a person's credit card information to make purchases or withdraw funds.
   - **Loan Scams**: Offers of low-interest loans that require upfront fees, which are never refunded once the loan fails to materialize.

The Impact of Scams

The impact of scams extends beyond financial loss, affecting victims emotionally and psychologically. The consequences of falling victim to a scam can be severe and long-lasting, including:

1. **Financial Loss**
   - Scams can result in significant financial losses, depleting victims' savings and leaving them in debt. For businesses, scams can lead to substantial financial setbacks and even bankruptcy.

2. **Emotional Distress**
   - Victims often experience a range of emotions, including anger, shame, guilt, and

helplessness. The sense of betrayal and violation can have profound psychological effects, leading to anxiety, depression, and loss of trust in others.

3. **Damage to Reputation**
   - For individuals and businesses, falling victim to a scam can harm their reputation. Personal relationships may suffer, and businesses may lose the trust of their customers and partners.

4. **Legal and Security Risks**
   - Scams involving identity theft can lead to further criminal activities, such as fraudulent loans or purchases made in the victim's name. This can result in legal complications and damage to the victim's credit score.

Societal Implications

Beyond the individual impact, scams have broader societal implications. They contribute to a culture of mistrust and can strain the resources of organizations and governments dedicated to combating fraud. The economic cost of scams is substantial, with billions of dollars lost annually. This financial drain affects not only the victims but also the economy at large, as resources that could be used for productive purposes are diverted to address the consequences of scams.

The Importance of Education and Vigilance

Given the pervasive nature of scams and their profound impact, education and vigilance are critical. By understanding the various types of scams and their warning signs, individuals can better protect themselves and their communities. This book aims to provide readers with the knowledge and tools necessary to recognize and avoid scams, fostering a culture of awareness and proactivity.

In the following chapters, we will delve deeper into the specifics of different scam types, explore real-life examples, and offer practical advice on how to safeguard against fraudulent activities. Through education and a proactive approach, we can reduce the incidence of scams and mitigate their impact on individuals and society.

Importance of Awareness

In an increasingly interconnected world, awareness has become a vital defense mechanism against the myriad scams that pervade our lives. Awareness, in this context, encompasses a deep understanding of the methods, tactics, and psychological manipulations employed by scammers. It involves recognizing the potential threats posed by scams and taking proactive steps to avoid falling victim. The importance of awareness cannot be overstated, as it forms the foundation for both individual and collective security in the face of ever-evolving fraudulent schemes.

The Psychological Manipulation of Scams

At the heart of every scam lies psychological manipulation. Scammers are adept at exploiting human emotions and cognitive biases to achieve their objectives. They prey on emotions such as greed, fear, trust, and urgency. By understanding these psychological underpinnings, individuals can better recognize when they are being targeted.

Greed is a common target for scammers. Offers that promise substantial financial rewards with minimal effort tap into the natural human desire for wealth and success. These offers often come in the form of investment opportunities, lottery winnings, or lucrative business deals.

The allure of quick and easy money can cloud judgment, making it difficult to see the scam for what it is. Awareness of this tactic allows individuals to question offers that seem too good to be true, applying critical thinking to assess their legitimacy.

Fear is another powerful tool in a scammer's arsenal. Scammers often create scenarios that induce panic, prompting immediate action without thorough consideration. Examples include threats of legal action, imminent financial loss, or personal harm. By instilling fear, scammers can bypass rational decision-making processes, pushing victims to comply with their demands swiftly.

Recognizing this tactic can help individuals remain calm and deliberate, seeking verification before taking any action.

Trust is fundamental to human relationships, and scammers exploit this trust to their advantage. They may impersonate trusted entities such as banks, government agencies, or even friends and family members. By leveraging the credibility of these entities, scammers can extract sensitive information or money from their victims. Awareness of this tactic encourages individuals to verify the identity of the requester independently, ensuring they are not falling for an impersonation.

Urgency is often employed to pressure individuals into making hasty decisions. Scammers create a sense of immediacy, claiming that an opportunity will expire or a threat will materialize if immediate action is not taken. This urgency can prevent individuals from taking the time to verify the legitimacy of the request. Being aware of this tactic can prompt individuals to slow down and thoroughly evaluate the situation before responding.

The Economic Impact of Scams

Scams have a profound economic impact on both individuals and society as a whole. The financial losses incurred by victims can be devastating, depleting savings, and leading to debt and financial instability.

For businesses, scams can result in substantial financial setbacks, loss of customer trust, and even bankruptcy. The ripple effects of these losses extend beyond the immediate victims, affecting the broader economy.

Individuals who fall victim to scams often face long-term financial consequences. Savings intended for retirement, education, or other significant expenses can be wiped out in an instant. Recovering from such losses can take years, during which victims may struggle to regain their financial footing. Awareness of the potential financial impact underscores the importance of vigilance and skepticism when confronted with unsolicited offers or requests.

Businesses are also frequent targets of scams. Phishing attacks, invoice fraud, and business email compromise (BEC) scams are just a few examples of how scammers exploit companies. The financial losses from these scams can be substantial, impacting profitability and operational stability.

Additionally, businesses that fall victim to scams may suffer reputational damage, leading to a loss of customer trust and future revenue. Awareness and training within businesses are essential to mitigate these risks and protect both financial assets and reputation.

On a societal level, the aggregate financial losses from scams are staggering. According to the Federal Trade Commission (FTC), consumers reported losing over $3.3 billion to fraud in 2020 alone. These losses represent a significant drain on the economy, diverting resources that could otherwise be used for productive purposes. Awareness campaigns and public education initiatives are crucial in reducing the prevalence of scams and their economic impact.

Emotional and Psychological Consequences

The impact of scams extends beyond financial loss, affecting victims emotionally and psychologically. The sense of violation and betrayal experienced by scam victims can have profound and lasting effects on mental health. Feelings of shame, guilt, and helplessness are common, as victims grapple with the realization that they have been deceived.

Victims of scams often experience a range of negative emotions. Anger and frustration are common initial reactions, directed both at the scammer and at oneself for falling victim. These emotions can be compounded by shame and guilt, as victims may feel responsible for their misfortune. The societal stigma associated with being scammed can exacerbate these feelings, leading to isolation and withdrawal from social interactions.

The psychological impact of scams can also include anxiety and depression. The stress of financial loss and the uncertainty of potential identity theft or further victimization can lead to chronic anxiety. Victims may constantly worry about their financial security and personal safety.

Depression can result from the profound sense of loss and the erosion of trust in others. The combination of these factors can significantly diminish the quality of life for scam victims.

Awareness of the emotional and psychological consequences of scams is crucial in providing appropriate support to victims.

Understanding that these reactions are normal and that victims are not to blame can help reduce the stigma and encourage individuals to seek help. Support groups, counseling services, and community resources can provide much-needed assistance to those recovering from the impact of scams.

Legal and Security Risks

Scams involving identity theft pose significant legal and security risks to victims. Identity theft occurs when scammers obtain personal information such as Social Security numbers, bank account details, or credit card information. This information can be used to commit further fraudulent activities, such as opening new accounts, making unauthorized purchases, or applying for loans in the victim's name.

The consequences of identity theft can be severe and long-lasting. Victims may find themselves entangled in legal disputes over debts they did not incur or facing challenges in restoring their credit. The process of resolving identity theft can be time-consuming and stressful, requiring extensive documentation and communication with financial institutions, credit bureaus, and law enforcement agencies.

Awareness of the risks associated with identity theft underscores the importance of protecting personal information. Individuals should be cautious about sharing sensitive information online or over the phone, especially when unsolicited requests are made.

Utilizing security measures such as two-factor authentication, secure passwords, and credit monitoring services can help mitigate the risk of identity theft.

Businesses also face significant legal and security risks from scams. Data breaches resulting from phishing attacks or other forms of cybercrime can expose sensitive customer information, leading to legal liabilities and regulatory penalties. Companies must implement robust cybersecurity measures and educate employees on best practices for data protection. Awareness and training programs are essential components of a comprehensive security strategy, helping to safeguard both company assets and customer data.

The Role of Education in Scam Prevention

Education is a powerful tool in the fight against scams. By equipping individuals with the knowledge and skills to recognize and respond to scams, we can reduce the incidence and impact of fraudulent activities. Educational initiatives can take many forms, from public awareness campaigns to targeted training programs for specific populations.

Public awareness campaigns play a crucial role in disseminating information about common scams and how to avoid them. Government agencies, consumer protection organizations, and community groups can collaborate to raise awareness through media, social networks, and community events.

These campaigns can highlight current scam trends, provide tips for recognizing red flags, and encourage individuals to report suspicious activities.

Targeted training programs can address the specific needs of different populations. For example, seniors are often targeted by scams due to perceived vulnerability and lack of familiarity with digital technologies. Educational programs for seniors can focus on common scams that target this demographic, such as Medicare fraud, fake lottery winnings, and tech support scams. Providing practical tips and resources can help seniors protect themselves and report scams effectively.

Businesses can also benefit from targeted training programs. Employee training on cybersecurity best practices, recognizing phishing attempts, and responding to potential scams can significantly reduce the risk of falling victim to fraud. Regular training updates and simulated phishing exercises can reinforce good practices and keep security top of mind for employees.

Schools and educational institutions have a role to play in teaching digital literacy and online safety to young people. As digital natives, children and teenagers are increasingly exposed to online threats.

Integrating scam awareness into the curriculum can help students develop critical thinking skills and a cautious approach to online interactions. Teaching students about privacy settings, safe browsing habits, and the importance of verifying information can build a foundation of digital resilience.

Proactive Measures for Scam Prevention

While awareness is the first line of defense against scams, proactive measures are essential for comprehensive protection. These measures involve taking deliberate actions to safeguard personal and financial information, reducing the risk of falling victim to scams.

One of the most effective proactive measures is maintaining strong cybersecurity practices. This includes using complex, unique passwords for different accounts and changing them regularly. Password management tools can help individuals create and store secure passwords. Enabling two-factor authentication adds an extra layer of security, requiring verification through a second device or method.

Regular monitoring of financial accounts and credit reports is another crucial proactive measure. By keeping a close eye on account activity, individuals can quickly identify and address any unauthorized transactions. Credit monitoring services can alert users to changes in their credit report, such as new accounts opened in their name, allowing for prompt action to mitigate potential fraud.

Being cautious with personal information is vital in preventing identity theft. Individuals should be wary of sharing sensitive information online or over the phone, especially in response to unsolicited requests.

Shredding documents containing personal information before disposal can prevent identity theft from physical sources.

Phishing emails and fake websites are common tactics used by scammers to steal personal information. Individuals should be vigilant when receiving emails or messages that request sensitive information or urge immediate action.

Verifying the authenticity of the sender and the legitimacy of the request is crucial. Hovering over links to check the URL before clicking and avoiding downloading attachments from unknown sources can help prevent falling victim to phishing scams.

For businesses, implementing comprehensive cybersecurity policies and practices is essential. This includes regular software updates and patches, firewalls, antivirus programs, and intrusion detection systems. Conducting regular security audits and vulnerability assessments can identify potential weaknesses and areas for improvement.

Employee training on recognizing and responding to scams is a critical component of business security. Educating employees about the latest scam tactics and reinforcing the importance of cybersecurity best practices can create a culture of vigilance. Encouraging employees to report suspicious activities and providing clear procedures for doing so can help prevent scams from escalating.

The Collective Responsibility in Scam Prevention

Preventing scams is not just an individual responsibility but a collective one. Communities, organizations, and governments all play a role in creating an environment where scams are less likely to succeed. Collaboration and information sharing are key to effective scam prevention.

Community organizations can provide valuable resources and support to individuals, especially vulnerable populations such as seniors. Workshops, informational sessions, and support groups can help raise awareness and provide practical advice on avoiding scams. Encouraging community members to look out for one another and share information about potential scams can create a network of protection.

Businesses can collaborate with industry groups and regulatory bodies to stay informed about emerging scam trends and best practices for prevention. Sharing information about scam incidents and prevention strategies can help create a more resilient business environment. Participating in industry-wide initiatives and adhering to regulatory guidelines can further enhance protection against scams.

Governments have a crucial role in protecting consumers from scams through legislation, regulation, and enforcement. Establishing and enforcing laws that penalize fraudulent activities and protect consumer rights is essential.

Government agencies can also provide resources and support for scam victims, including hotlines, reporting mechanisms, and educational materials.

Public-private partnerships can enhance scam prevention efforts by combining the strengths and resources of both sectors. Collaborative initiatives can raise awareness, develop innovative solutions, and create a unified approach to combating scams.

Engaging in dialogue with stakeholders, including consumer groups, industry representatives, and law enforcement, can lead to more effective and comprehensive strategies for scam prevention.

The Path Forward: Building a Culture of Awareness

Building a culture of awareness requires ongoing effort and commitment from individuals, communities, and institutions. As scams continue to evolve, staying informed and vigilant is essential. This book aims to provide the foundation for understanding and recognizing scams, but the journey does not end here.

Individuals should continue to educate themselves and others about new scam tactics and prevention strategies. Staying updated on the latest developments in cybersecurity and fraud prevention can help maintain a high level of awareness. Sharing knowledge with family, friends, and colleagues can amplify the impact, creating a ripple effect of protection.

Communities can foster a culture of awareness by organizing events, workshops, and support groups focused on scam prevention. Encouraging open communication and information sharing can help community members stay informed and vigilant. Building strong networks of trust and support can enhance collective resilience against scams.

Businesses should prioritize ongoing training and education for employees, ensuring that they are equipped to recognize and respond to scams. Regularly reviewing and updating cybersecurity policies and practices can help maintain a robust defense against emerging threats. Engaging with industry groups and participating in collaborative initiatives can enhance business resilience.

Governments and regulatory bodies should continue to develop and enforce policies that protect consumers from scams. Providing resources and support for scam victims, conducting public awareness campaigns, and collaborating with private sector partners can enhance overall scam prevention efforts.

By building a culture of awareness, we can create a safer and more secure environment for everyone. The collective effort to recognize, avoid, and combat scams will reduce their prevalence and impact, protecting individuals and communities from the harmful consequences of fraud. Through education, vigilance, and proactive measures, we can empower ourselves and others to stay one step ahead of scammers and safeguard our personal and financial well-being.

CHAPTER 1
UNDERSTANDING SCAMS

Definition and Types of Scams

Scams are deceitful schemes designed to fraudulently obtain money, personal information, or other assets from unsuspecting individuals. These schemes often rely on exploiting human psychology and the trust inherent in social interactions. As technology has advanced, so have the methods and sophistication of scams. Today, scams can occur through various channels, including online, over the phone, in person, and via mail. This chapter delves into the myriad types of scams, with a particular focus on online scams, given their prevalence and the significant threat they pose in our digital age.

Online Scams

The rise of the internet has revolutionized communication, commerce, and access to information, but it has also provided fertile ground for scammers to operate. Online scams are particularly insidious because they can reach millions of potential victims with minimal effort and cost to the scammer. These scams often involve complex tactics designed to deceive individuals into providing personal information, transferring money, or engaging in fraudulent transactions. Understanding the various forms of online scams and the tactics employed by scammers is crucial for safeguarding oneself against these threats.

Phishing

Phishing is one of the most common and well-known forms of online scams. It involves scammers sending emails, messages, or even creating websites that appear to be from legitimate, trusted sources, such as banks, social media platforms, or government agencies. The primary objective of phishing is to trick individuals into providing sensitive information, such as usernames, passwords, credit card numbers, or social security numbers.

Phishing emails often create a sense of urgency, suggesting that immediate action is required to avoid negative consequences. For example, an email may claim that there has been suspicious activity on your bank account and prompt you to click a link to verify your identity. This link typically leads to a fake website that closely mimics the legitimate site, designed to capture your login credentials when you enter them.

Phishing attacks can be highly targeted, known as spear phishing, where the scammer customizes the message to a specific individual or organization, increasing the likelihood of success. For instance, a spear-phishing email might address the recipient by name and reference specific details about their job or personal life, making it appear more authentic.

To protect against phishing, it is essential to be cautious with unsolicited emails and messages, especially those requesting personal information or urging immediate action. Verifying the legitimacy of the communication by contacting the organization directly through official channels, rather than using links or contact information provided in the suspicious message, is a critical step in avoiding phishing scams.

Fake Websites

Fake websites, also known as spoofed or fraudulent websites, are another common tactic used in online scams. These websites are designed to look identical or very similar to legitimate sites, with the intention of deceiving visitors into entering sensitive information. Fake websites can be part of a phishing campaign, where the scammer directs victims to the site through emails or messages, or they can be standalone operations targeting individuals through search engines or social media ads.

Creating a fake website often involves replicating the design, logos, and content of the legitimate site. Scammers may use domain names that closely resemble the authentic website, with slight variations that can be easily overlooked (e.g., using "arnazon.com" instead of "amazon.com"). These sites can capture personal information, login credentials, and payment details entered by unsuspecting visitors.

To avoid falling victim to fake websites, it is important to pay close attention to the URL and ensure it matches the legitimate site exactly. Using bookmarks for frequently visited sites and typing the URL directly into the browser rather than clicking on links can also help. Additionally, checking for security indicators such as HTTPS and the padlock icon in the browser address bar can provide some assurance that the site is secure.

Social Media Scams

Social media platforms have become a significant venue for scams, leveraging the vast reach and social trust inherent in these networks. Scammers can exploit social media in various ways, including creating fake profiles, hacking legitimate accounts, and using social engineering tactics to deceive users.

Fake profiles are often used to befriend individuals and build trust over time, eventually leading to requests for money or personal information. These profiles may impersonate real people or create fictitious identities with appealing personas. Once a connection is established, the scammer may claim to be in urgent need of financial assistance due to an emergency or offer lucrative investment opportunities.

Hacked accounts, where scammers gain control of a legitimate user's social media profile, can also be used to perpetrate scams. By posing as a trusted friend or family member, scammers can send messages requesting financial help or promoting fraudulent links and offers. These messages are more likely to be believed because they appear to come from someone the victim knows personally.

Social engineering tactics involve manipulating individuals into divulging personal information or performing actions that compromise their security. For example, a scammer might create a post or message claiming to offer free products, discounts, or exclusive access in exchange for completing a survey or sharing a post. These interactions can lead to the collection of personal data or the spread of malicious links.

To protect against social media scams, users should be cautious about accepting friend requests from unknown individuals, even if they have mutual connections. It is also important to verify the identity of anyone requesting money or personal information, particularly if the request seems out of character. Using strong, unique passwords for social media accounts and enabling two-factor authentication can help secure accounts against hacking attempts.

E-commerce Scams

The convenience of online shopping has made e-commerce a booming industry, but it has also created opportunities for scams. E-commerce scams can take various forms, including fake online stores, counterfeit products, and fraudulent payment schemes.

Fake online stores are designed to mimic legitimate retailers, offering attractive prices on popular products to lure in unsuspecting shoppers. These sites often have professional-looking designs and may even include fake reviews and testimonials to build credibility. Once a purchase is made, the victim may receive counterfeit goods, inferior products, or nothing at all.

Counterfeit products are a significant issue in e-commerce, with scammers selling fake versions of branded items at discounted prices. These products can range from electronics and fashion items to pharmaceuticals and cosmetics. Not only do victims lose money, but they may also receive items that are of poor quality or even dangerous.

Fraudulent payment schemes involve manipulating the payment process to defraud the buyer. For example, a scammer might request payment through untraceable methods such as wire transfers, gift cards, or cryptocurrency. These payment methods are often irreversible, making it difficult for victims to recover their money. Additionally, scammers may use techniques such as "carding," where stolen credit card information is used to make purchases.

To avoid e-commerce scams, it is important to shop from reputable and well-known online retailers. Checking for customer reviews, verifying contact information, and looking for secure payment methods can help ensure the legitimacy of an online store. Avoiding deals that seem too good to be true and being cautious with unfamiliar websites can also reduce the risk of falling victim to these scams.

Romance Scams

Romance scams exploit the desire for companionship and love, preying on individuals seeking relationships through online dating sites and social media platforms. Scammers create fake profiles, often using stolen photos and fabricated details, to build a connection with their victims over time. The goal is to establish trust and emotional intimacy, eventually leading to requests for money or personal information.

Romance scammers often weave elaborate stories to explain their need for financial assistance. Common scenarios include claiming to be working overseas, facing an emergency, or needing funds to visit the victim in person. These stories are designed to elicit sympathy and a sense of urgency, prompting the victim to send money.

The emotional manipulation involved in romance scams can be profound, leaving victims feeling betrayed and heartbroken. The financial losses can also be significant, as victims may be persuaded to send large sums of money over the course of the relationship.

To protect against romance scams, it is important to be cautious when interacting with individuals met online, particularly if they quickly profess strong feelings or ask for money. Verifying the identity of the person through video calls, social media profiles, and other means can help confirm their legitimacy. Being aware of common red flags, such as inconsistent details in their stories or reluctance to meet in person, can also help identify potential scams.

Employment Scams

Employment scams take advantage of individuals seeking job opportunities, often targeting those who are unemployed or underemployed. These scams can appear in various forms, including fake job listings, fraudulent recruitment agencies, and work-from-home schemes.

Fake job listings are posted on job boards, social media, and classified ad websites, advertising attractive positions with competitive salaries and benefits. Once an individual applies, they may be asked to provide personal information, such as their Social Security number, banking details, or a copy of their ID, under the guise of conducting background checks or setting up direct deposit. This information can then be used for identity theft.

Fraudulent recruitment agencies charge job seekers upfront fees for their services, promising to find them high-paying jobs. After paying the fee, the job seeker may receive little or no assistance, or the jobs they are offered may not exist.

Work-from-home schemes often promise easy money for minimal effort, such as stuffing envelopes, assembling products, or processing payments. In reality, these schemes may require the victim to pay for materials or training, with little or no compensation in return. Some work-from-home scams involve money laundering, where the victim is unwittingly recruited to process stolen funds.

To avoid employment scams, it is important to research the company and the job listing thoroughly. Legitimate employers typically do not require personal information or payment upfront. Checking for reviews and testimonials, verifying contact information, and being cautious of job offers that seem too good to be true can help identify potential scams.

Tech Support Scams

Tech support scams prey on individuals' fears of computer viruses and technical issues. Scammers pose as technical support representatives from reputable companies, such as Microsoft or Apple, and claim that the victim's computer is infected with malware or experiencing other problems. These scams can be initiated through unsolicited phone calls, pop-up messages, or fake websites.

Once the scammer convinces the victim that their computer is compromised, they may request remote access to fix the issue. During the remote session, the scammer can install malware, steal personal information, or manipulate the computer to display fake error messages. They may also demand payment for their "services," often through untraceable methods such as gift cards or cryptocurrency.

To protect against tech support scams, it is important to be skeptical of unsolicited calls or messages claiming to be from tech support. Reputable companies do not typically initiate contact with customers in this manner. If a pop-up message or website claims that your computer is infected, do not call the provided phone number or click on any links. Instead, contact the official support channels of the software or device manufacturer directly.

Investment Scams

Investment scams entice individuals with the promise of high returns on investments, often with little or no risk. These scams can take various forms, including Ponzi schemes, pyramid schemes, and fraudulent investment opportunities.

Ponzi schemes involve paying returns to earlier investors using the contributions of newer investors. These schemes rely on a constant influx of new investors to sustain the payouts, and they eventually collapse when the scammer can no longer recruit enough new participants. Victims of Ponzi schemes often lose their entire investment when the scheme collapses.

Pyramid schemes involve recruiting new participants to invest in the scheme, with the promise of earning money through the recruitment of additional participants. These schemes are unsustainable because they require exponential growth in the number of participants to continue paying returns. Like Ponzi schemes, pyramid schemes eventually collapse, leaving the majority of participants with significant losses.

Fraudulent investment opportunities can involve fake stocks, bonds, or other financial instruments. Scammers may create professional-looking websites, marketing materials, and even fake regulatory approvals to convince victims of the legitimacy of the investment. Once the victim invests their money, the scammer disappears, leaving the victim with worthless assets.

To avoid investment scams, it is important to thoroughly research any investment opportunity and the individuals or companies promoting it. Checking for regulatory registration, verifying contact information, and seeking independent financial advice can help identify legitimate investments. Being wary of promises of high returns with little or no risk is also crucial, as legitimate investments typically carry some level of risk.

Lottery and Prize Scams

Lottery and prize scams lure victims with the promise of winning a significant prize, such as cash, a car, or a vacation. The scammer contacts the victim, often through email, phone, or mail, and claims that they have won a lottery or sweepstakes. To claim the prize, the victim is instructed to pay fees or taxes upfront, provide personal information, or call a premium-rate phone number.

In reality, there is no prize, and the victim's money or information is stolen. Lottery and prize scams often use the names and logos of legitimate lotteries or sweepstakes to appear credible. They may also create a sense of urgency, claiming that the prize must be claimed within a short timeframe.

To avoid lottery and prize scams, it is important to remember that legitimate lotteries and sweepstakes do not require payment or personal information to claim a prize. If you receive a notification of a prize win that you did not enter, it is likely a scam. Verifying the legitimacy of the prize with the official organization and avoiding any requests for upfront payments can help protect against these scams.

Charity Scams

Charity scams exploit individuals' generosity and desire to help others, particularly during times of crisis or disaster. Scammers pose as representatives of legitimate charities or create fake charitable organizations to solicit donations. These scams can occur through phone calls, emails, social media, or in-person solicitations.

Charity scams often use emotional appeals to elicit donations, such as stories of individuals in need, photos of disaster-affected areas, or urgent requests for aid. The donations collected are not used for charitable purposes but are instead pocketed by the scammer.

To protect against charity scams, it is important to verify the legitimacy of the charity before making a donation. Checking for registration with official charity watchdog organizations, reviewing the charity's financial statements, and contacting the charity directly through official channels can help ensure that donations are used for their intended purpose. Being cautious of unsolicited requests for donations and avoiding cash donations can also reduce the risk of falling victim to charity scams.

Ransomware

Ransomware is a type of malware that encrypts the victim's files, rendering them inaccessible. The scammer then demands a ransom, usually in cryptocurrency, to provide the decryption key. Ransomware attacks can be initiated through phishing emails, malicious downloads, or vulnerabilities in software and systems.

The impact of ransomware can be devastating, as victims may lose access to critical data, such as personal documents, business records, or financial information. Paying the ransom does not guarantee that the files will be restored, and it may encourage further attacks.

To protect against ransomware, it is important to maintain

regular backups of important files, use robust security software, and keep systems and software updated with the latest patches. Being cautious of unsolicited emails and avoiding downloading attachments or clicking on links from unknown sources can help prevent ransomware infections.

Cryptocurrency Scams

Cryptocurrency scams have become increasingly prevalent with the rise of digital currencies such as Bitcoin, Ethereum, and others. These scams can take various forms, including fake initial coin offerings (ICOs), Ponzi schemes, and phishing attacks targeting cryptocurrency wallets.

Fake ICOs involve creating a new cryptocurrency or token and promoting it as a lucrative investment opportunity. Scammers may create professional-looking websites, whitepapers, and marketing materials to convince investors of the legitimacy of the project. Once the funds are raised, the scammer disappears, leaving investors with worthless tokens.

Ponzi schemes in the cryptocurrency space operate similarly to traditional Ponzi schemes, with early investors being paid returns from the contributions of new investors. These schemes rely on continuous recruitment of new participants and eventually collapse, leaving most investors with significant losses.

Phishing attacks targeting cryptocurrency wallets involve scammers creating fake websites or sending emails that mimic legitimate cryptocurrency exchanges or wallet providers. The goal is to trick individuals into entering their login credentials or private keys, allowing the scammer to steal their cryptocurrency.

To protect against cryptocurrency scams, it is important to thoroughly research any investment opportunity and the individuals or companies promoting it. Verifying the legitimacy of the project, checking for regulatory compliance, and using secure methods to store and manage cryptocurrency can help reduce the risk of falling victim to these scams. Being cautious of unsolicited offers and avoiding sharing private keys or login credentials can also enhance security.

Online scams are a pervasive and evolving threat in today's digital age. By understanding the various types of scams and the tactics used by scammers, individuals can better protect themselves and their personal information. Awareness, vigilance, and proactive measures are essential components of a robust defense against online fraud. As technology continues to advance, staying informed about new and emerging scam tactics will be crucial in maintaining security and safeguarding against fraudulent activities.

Psychology of Scams

Scams are not just about the mechanics of deceit; they delve deeply into the psychological fabric of human behavior. Understanding the psychology behind scams provides crucial insights into why individuals fall victim to them, despite often having the knowledge and resources to avoid such pitfalls. This section explores the cognitive biases, emotional triggers, and social dynamics that scammers exploit to achieve their malicious goals.

Cognitive Biases and Heuristics

Human decision-making is influenced by a variety of cognitive biases and heuristics—mental shortcuts that help people make judgments quickly. While these shortcuts can be useful in everyday life, they can also be exploited by scammers.

One of the most commonly exploited cognitive biases is **confirmation bias**. This bias leads individuals to seek out, interpret, and remember information that confirms their pre-existing beliefs while disregarding information that contradicts them. Scammers craft their messages and scenarios to align with the victim's expectations and desires, making it easier for the scam to seem plausible. For example, a phishing email that mimics a notification from a popular bank exploits the recipient's existing trust in that institution.

Authority bias is another powerful tool for scammers. This bias causes individuals to attribute greater accuracy to the opinion of an authority figure and be more influenced by that opinion. Scammers often impersonate figures of authority—such as bank officials, government agents, or technical support personnel—to lend credibility to their deceit. When individuals perceive that the message is coming from an authoritative source, they are more likely to comply without questioning its validity.

The **scarcity heuristic** suggests that people place a higher value on things that are perceived to be in limited supply. This principle is frequently used in scams to create a sense of urgency. Limited-time offers, threats of account closures, or claims of exclusive opportunities all play on the fear of missing out, prompting individuals to act quickly and without due diligence.

Reciprocity is another psychological principle that scammers exploit. This principle holds that people are more likely to comply with a request from someone who has done them a favor. Scammers might offer a small token or free service to create a sense of obligation in the victim. Once the victim feels indebted, they are more likely to comply with subsequent requests, such as providing personal information or making a payment.

Emotional Triggers

Scammers are adept at manipulating emotions to achieve their ends. Emotional triggers are powerful because they can override rational thought processes, making individuals more susceptible to deception.

Fear is a common emotion that scammers exploit. By creating scenarios that evoke fear—such as threats of legal action, financial loss, or personal harm—scammers can induce panic in their victims. In a state of fear, individuals are less likely to scrutinize the legitimacy of the threat and more likely to comply with the scammer's demands. For instance, a scammer posing as an IRS agent might threaten the victim with immediate arrest for unpaid taxes, prompting the victim to pay a fraudulent fee to avoid the purported consequences.

Greed is another emotion that scammers frequently target. The promise of easy money, high returns on investments, or winning a lottery can be enticing. These offers appeal to the victim's desire for financial gain, clouding their judgment and making them overlook the warning signs of a scam. Investment scams and advance-fee frauds often leverage this emotional trigger to lure victims into parting with their money.

Sympathy and compassion are emotions that can also be manipulated. Scammers may create stories of hardship, illness, or urgent need to elicit a sympathetic response from their victims. Romance scams and charity frauds often rely on building emotional connections and exploiting the victim's desire to help others. By appealing to the victim's sense of empathy, scammers can extract money or personal information under the guise of needing assistance.

Excitement and curiosity can also make individuals vulnerable to scams. Offers of exclusive deals, secret information, or rare opportunities can pique interest and lead individuals to take risks they might otherwise avoid. Scammers use this to their advantage by creating enticing narratives that compel the victim to act quickly, without thorough consideration.

Social Dynamics and Influence

Social dynamics and the influence of others play a significant role in how scams succeed. Scammers often use social proof, conformity, and trust to manipulate their victims.

Social proof is the psychological phenomenon where people assume the actions of others in an attempt to reflect correct behavior in a given situation. Scammers exploit this by creating fake testimonials, endorsements, and reviews to lend credibility to their schemes. Seeing that others have supposedly benefited from the offer can make the scam seem more legitimate and encourage victims to participate.

Conformity refers to the tendency of individuals to align their attitudes, beliefs, and behaviors with those of a group. Scammers leverage this by creating scenarios where the victim feels pressured to conform to the expectations of the group. For example, in a pyramid scheme, the victim may be influenced by the apparent success of others in the group and feel compelled to invest and recruit new members to fit in.

Trust is a fundamental component of social interactions, and scammers work hard to build and then exploit it. They often pose as trustworthy individuals or entities—such as friends, family members, or reputable organizations—to gain the victim's confidence. Once trust is established, victims are more likely to comply with requests for money, personal information, or access to accounts.

Reciprocal liking is another social dynamic that scammers use. This principle suggests that people tend to like and trust those who express liking or admiration for them. Scammers, especially in romance scams, often shower their victims with compliments, affection, and attention to create a sense of mutual liking. This emotional bond can lower the victim's defenses and make them more susceptible to manipulation.

The Role of Technology in Modern Scams

Technology has amplified the reach and effectiveness of scams, providing scammers with new tools and methods to deceive their victims. Understanding the technological aspects of scams is crucial in recognizing and preventing them.

Email and instant messaging have become primary channels for phishing and other online scams. These platforms allow scammers to reach a large audience with minimal effort and cost. Advanced techniques such as email spoofing and domain squatting make it easier for scammers to create convincing messages that appear to come from legitimate sources. The anonymity provided by these digital channels also makes it harder to trace and apprehend scammers.

Social media has transformed the landscape of scams by providing scammers with a wealth of personal information about their potential victims. Through social engineering, scammers can gather details about individuals' interests, relationships, and activities, crafting highly targeted and personalized scams. Fake profiles and hacked accounts are common tools used to build trust and credibility on social media platforms.

Cryptocurrencies have introduced new opportunities for financial scams. The relative anonymity and irreversible nature of cryptocurrency transactions make them an attractive medium for scammers. Ponzi schemes, fake ICOs, and ransomware attacks often demand payment in cryptocurrencies, complicating the process of tracing and recovering funds.

Deepfakes and AI are emerging technologies that pose significant challenges in the realm of scams. Deepfake technology can create realistic but fake videos and audio recordings, making it easier for scammers to impersonate trusted individuals. AI can be used to automate phishing attacks, analyze victims' behavior, and refine scamming techniques for higher success rates.

Malware and ransomware continue to be major threats. Scammers use malware to steal personal information, monitor activities, and control victims' devices. Ransomware attacks, where the victim's data is encrypted and held for ransom, have become increasingly sophisticated and damaging.

To combat these technologically advanced scams, individuals must stay informed about the latest threats and adopt robust cybersecurity practices. Regular updates to software, strong passwords, multi-factor authentication, and cautious behavior online are essential components of a defensive strategy.

Case Studies: Illustrating the Psychology of Scams

Real-world examples help illustrate how scammers exploit psychological principles to deceive their victims. Examining these case studies provides valuable lessons and insights into how scams operate and how to avoid them.

One notable case is the **Nigerian Prince** scam, also known as the

419 scam. This scam typically involves an email from someone claiming to be a Nigerian prince or government official who needs help transferring a large sum of money out of the country. In return for the victim's assistance, they promise a substantial reward. The scam exploits greed and authority bias, as the email appears to come from a high-ranking official and offers a lucrative payoff. Victims who respond are asked to pay various fees to facilitate the transfer, which continue to escalate until the victim realizes they have been duped.

Another example is the **Tech Support** scam, where victims receive unsolicited calls from individuals claiming to be from tech companies like Microsoft or Apple. The scammer asserts that the victim's computer is infected with a virus or has some other issue that needs immediate attention. Fear and authority bias are key psychological levers here. The victim, worried about the security of their device and trusting the supposed authority of the tech company, grants remote access to the scammer. This access allows the scammer to install malware, steal personal information, or demand payment for unnecessary or nonexistent services.

The **Grandparent** scam preys on the elderly, exploiting their love and concern for their family. In this scam, the victim receives a call from someone claiming to be their grandchild in distress, needing money urgently for bail, medical expenses, or other emergencies. The scammer may have gathered personal information about the family to make the call more convincing. The emotional trigger of fear for a loved one's safety and the urgency to help prompt the victim to send money quickly, often through untraceable methods.

The **Romance** scam, often perpetrated through online dating sites, is a prime example of how trust and emotional manipulation are used. Scammers create fake profiles to woo victims, building a relationship over weeks or months. Once trust and affection are established, the scammer fabricates a crisis—such as a medical emergency or travel mishap—and asks for financial help. The victim, emotionally invested in the relationship, is more likely to comply, sometimes losing substantial amounts of money before realizing the deceit.

Psychological Resilience and Scam Prevention

Building psychological resilience is crucial in preventing scams. Understanding the psychological tactics used by scammers can help individuals recognize and resist these manipulations. Several strategies can enhance psychological resilience and reduce susceptibility to scams.

Critical thinking is a vital skill in scam prevention. By questioning and analyzing the information presented, individuals can identify inconsistencies and red flags. Developing a habit of verifying the legitimacy of offers and requests, especially those that seem too good to be true, can prevent hasty decisions based on emotional reactions.

Emotional regulation helps individuals manage their responses to fear, excitement, or urgency. Techniques such as mindfulness, stress management, and taking time to consider decisions can mitigate the impact of emotional triggers. By maintaining a calm and measured approach, individuals can better assess the situation and avoid impulsive actions.

Education and awareness are foundational components of resilience. Staying informed about common scams and how they operate provides a defense against deception. Educational programs, public awareness campaigns, and resources from consumer protection agencies can equip individuals with the knowledge needed to identify and avoid scams.

Support networks play a crucial role in scam prevention and recovery. Discussing suspicious offers or requests with trusted friends, family, or colleagues can provide additional perspectives and help identify potential scams. For victims of scams, support networks can offer emotional support and practical assistance in dealing with the aftermath.

Assertiveness and confidence in saying no can protect individuals from high-pressure tactics. Scammers often rely on creating a sense of urgency or authority to push victims into compliance. Being confident in one's ability to refuse requests for personal information or money, and seeking verification from independent sources, can disrupt the scammer's strategy.

The Role of Institutions in Preventing Scams

While individual awareness and resilience are critical, institutions also play a significant role in preventing scams. Businesses, financial institutions, and government agencies can implement measures to protect their clients and contribute to broader scam prevention efforts.

Businesses can educate their customers about common scams and how to avoid them. Providing clear communication about company policies, such as never requesting personal information via email or phone, can help customers recognize fraudulent attempts. Implementing robust security measures, such as multi-factor authentication and secure payment processes, can also reduce the risk of scams.

Financial institutions are on the front lines of scam prevention. Banks and credit card companies can monitor for unusual account activity and alert customers to potential fraud. Offering resources and tools for customers to secure their accounts, such as transaction alerts and fraud detection services, can enhance protection. Financial institutions can also collaborate with law enforcement to identify and shut down fraudulent operations.

Government agencies have a crucial role in regulating and enforcing laws against scams. Establishing and enforcing consumer protection laws, investigating fraud, and prosecuting scammers are essential functions. Government agencies can also lead public awareness campaigns, providing information on how to recognize and report scams. Collaboration with international agencies is important in addressing cross-border scams and enhancing global efforts to combat fraud.

Future Trends in Scams and Scam Prevention

As technology and society continue to evolve, so do the tactics and methods of scammers. Anticipating future trends in scams can help individuals and institutions stay ahead of emerging threats and develop effective prevention strategies.

Artificial Intelligence (AI) and machine learning are likely to be leveraged by scammers to create more sophisticated and convincing scams. AI can analyze vast amounts of data to personalize scam messages, making them more relevant and believable to each target. Deepfake technology, which creates realistic but fake audio and video, can be used to impersonate trusted individuals, adding another layer of deception.

Cybersecurity advancements will continue to play a crucial role in scam prevention. Developing and deploying advanced security technologies, such as biometric authentication and blockchain, can enhance protection against fraud. However, as cybersecurity measures become more sophisticated, scammers will also adapt, necessitating ongoing vigilance and innovation.

Global collaboration in fighting scams will become increasingly important. Scammers often operate across borders, making it challenging for individual countries to address the issue effectively. International cooperation, including information sharing, joint investigations, and coordinated enforcement actions, will be essential in combating global scams.

Public awareness and education will remain foundational in scam prevention. As new scams emerge, continuous efforts to educate the public about these threats and how to avoid them will be necessary. Leveraging digital platforms and social media to reach a wide audience can enhance the effectiveness of awareness campaigns.

The psychology of scams is complex and multifaceted, involving cognitive biases, emotional triggers, and social dynamics. By understanding these psychological principles, individuals can better recognize and resist the tactics used by scammers. Building psychological resilience, staying informed, and adopting proactive measures are essential components of scam prevention.

Institutions also play a vital role in protecting individuals from scams. Businesses, financial institutions, and government agencies must implement robust security measures, educate their customers, and enforce consumer protection laws. Anticipating future trends in scams and adapting prevention strategies accordingly will be crucial in maintaining security in an ever-evolving landscape.

Ultimately, combating scams requires a collective effort. By fostering a culture of awareness, vigilance, and resilience, we can reduce the prevalence and impact of scams, protecting individuals and communities from the harmful consequences of fraud.

Common Scamming Techniques

Scams are pervasive, affecting millions of individuals and businesses worldwide. Understanding the common techniques used by scammers is crucial for safeguarding oneself and others. This chapter explores several prevalent scamming methods, including phishing, bait and switch, and impersonation, delving into how they operate and how to recognize and avoid them.

Phishing

Phishing is one of the most widespread and damaging scamming techniques, primarily because of its versatility and effectiveness. Phishing involves sending deceptive communications—typically emails, but also text messages, social media messages, or even phone calls—designed to trick recipients into divulging sensitive information, such as usernames, passwords, credit card numbers, or other personal data.

Phishing attacks rely heavily on social engineering tactics, manipulating victims' trust and emotions. These messages often appear to come from reputable organizations, such as banks, online retailers, or government agencies. The content is crafted to instill a sense of urgency or fear, prompting the recipient to act quickly without thoroughly scrutinizing the legitimacy of the request.

One common form of phishing is the **email phishing attack**. In these attacks, the scammer sends an email that appears to be from a trusted entity. The email typically contains a message indicating that there is a problem with the recipient's account or that immediate action is required to prevent negative consequences. For example, an email might claim that the recipient's bank account has been compromised and that they need to click a link to verify their information. This link leads to a fake website designed to look like the legitimate one, where the victim is prompted to enter their login credentials. Once these credentials are entered, they are captured by the scammer and used to access the victim's real account.

Another variant of phishing is **spear phishing**, a more targeted form of attack. Unlike general phishing, which is sent to a broad audience, spear phishing targets specific individuals or organizations. The messages are often personalized, using information gathered from social media profiles or other public sources to make the email seem more credible. For example, a spear-phishing email might reference a recent business transaction or use the recipient's name and position within the company. Because these emails are highly customized, they are more convincing and have a higher success rate.

Whaling is a type of spear phishing that targets high-profile individuals, such as executives or senior managers within an organization. These attacks are meticulously crafted and often involve significant research to gather detailed information about the target. The goal is to deceive the individual into performing actions that compromise the organization's security, such as transferring large sums of money or providing sensitive information.

Another form of phishing is **clone phishing**, where the scammer creates a nearly identical copy of a legitimate email that the victim has previously received. The cloned email contains malicious links or attachments and is sent from an address that appears very similar to the original sender's. Because the email looks familiar and expected, the victim is more likely to trust it and follow the instructions.

Vishing (voice phishing) and **smishing** (SMS phishing) are variations that use phone calls and text messages, respectively, to deceive victims. In vishing, the scammer might call the victim, pretending to be from their bank or another trusted organization, and ask for personal information to "verify" the victim's identity. Smishing involves sending text messages that contain links to phishing websites or prompt the recipient to call a fraudulent phone number.

To protect against phishing, individuals should be cautious of unsolicited messages that request personal information or urge immediate action. Verifying the authenticity of the communication by contacting the organization directly using official contact details is a critical step. Additionally, being aware of the common signs of phishing—such as generic greetings, poor grammar, and suspicious links—can help individuals recognize and avoid these scams.

Bait and Switch

Bait and switch is another common scamming technique that exploits the expectations and desires of victims. This method involves advertising a desirable product or service at an attractive price (the bait) to lure potential buyers. However, when the victim attempts to purchase the advertised item, they are presented with a different, often inferior, product or service (the switch). This technique is frequently used in both online and offline settings and can take various forms.

In retail settings, bait and switch scams often occur in sales promotions. A store might advertise a high-demand product, such as a popular electronic device, at a very low price to attract customers. When customers visit the store, they are informed that the item is out of stock and are instead offered a different, often more expensive or lower-quality product. The goal is to entice customers into the store with the bait and then upsell them on other items.

Online, bait and switch scams are commonly seen on e-commerce platforms and classified ad websites. Scammers create listings for sought-after items at unbeatable prices to attract buyers. Once the buyer expresses interest and attempts to make the purchase, the scammer either delivers a substandard product or claims that the advertised item is no longer available and offers an alternative product. In some cases, the scammer may take the buyer's money and deliver nothing at all.

Real estate is another area where bait and switch tactics are prevalent. Scammers might advertise rental properties or homes for sale at below-market prices to attract potential tenants or buyers. When the victim contacts the scammer, they are told that the property is no longer available and are directed to a different property, which may have significantly different terms or conditions. This tactic exploits the victim's desire for a good deal and can lead to financial loss and wasted time.

In the service industry, bait and switch scams can occur when companies advertise a particular service at a low rate. Once the customer engages with the company, they are informed that the advertised rate does not cover all aspects of the service, and additional fees are required. For example, a moving company might quote a low price for their services but then add extra charges for packing materials, stairs, or heavy items once the move is underway.

To avoid bait and switch scams, consumers should be wary of offers that seem too good to be true. Researching the seller or service provider, reading reviews, and verifying the terms and conditions of the offer can help identify potential scams. Additionally, consumers should be cautious of high-pressure sales tactics that push them to make quick decisions without sufficient information.

Impersonation

Impersonation is a scamming technique where the scammer pretends to be someone else, often a trusted individual or representative of a reputable organization. This method relies on the inherent trust that victims have in the person or organization being impersonated. By convincing the victim of their legitimacy, the scammer can extract money, personal information, or other valuable assets.

Impersonation scams can take many forms, including fake phone calls, emails, or in-person interactions. One common example is the **imposter scam**, where the scammer poses as a government official, such as an IRS agent or law enforcement officer. The scammer contacts the victim, claiming that they owe taxes or have committed a crime, and demands immediate payment to avoid arrest or legal action. These scams often use fear and intimidation to pressure the victim into compliance.

Business email compromise (BEC) is another form of impersonation scam that targets companies and organizations. In a BEC attack, the scammer gains access to a legitimate email account within the organization, often through phishing or hacking. The scammer then uses this account to send fraudulent emails to employees, vendors, or customers, requesting payments or sensitive information. Because the email appears to come from a trusted source within the organization, the recipients are more likely to comply without suspicion.

Romance scams also frequently involve impersonation. Scammers create fake online profiles on dating sites or social media platforms, posing as attractive and interested individuals. They build a relationship with the victim over time, gaining their trust and affection. Once the emotional connection is established, the scammer fabricates a crisis or emergency and asks for financial assistance. The victim, believing they are helping a loved one, may send money or provide personal information, only to discover that the entire relationship was a sham.

Tech support scams involve scammers posing as technical support representatives from well-known companies like Microsoft or Apple. The scammer contacts the victim, claiming that their computer is infected with a virus or has a technical issue that needs immediate attention. They then instruct the victim to provide remote access to their computer or to purchase unnecessary software or services. Once the scammer gains access, they can steal personal information, install malware, or demand payment for bogus repairs.

CEO fraud is a specific type of BEC where the scammer impersonates a high-ranking executive within the organization, such as the CEO or CFO. The scammer sends an urgent email to an employee, typically someone in the finance department, instructing them to transfer funds to a specified account. The email often stresses the need for confidentiality and quick action, making the request seem legitimate and pressing.

Family and friend impersonation scams involve the scammer posing as a relative or close friend in distress. They may contact the victim via phone, email, or social media, claiming to be in an emergency situation and needing immediate financial help. The scammer might say they are stranded in a foreign country, facing legal trouble, or experiencing a medical emergency. The victim, wanting to help their loved one, sends money or provides personal information without verifying the authenticity of the request.

To protect against impersonation scams, individuals should be cautious of unsolicited requests for money or personal information, even if they appear to come from a trusted source. Verifying the identity of the requester through independent means, such as calling a known phone number or speaking in person, can help confirm the legitimacy of the request. Being aware of the common signs of impersonation scams—such as high-pressure tactics, requests for secrecy, and unusual payment methods—can also help individuals recognize and avoid these threats.

The Mechanics of Scamming Techniques

While the specific methods used in phishing, bait and switch, and impersonation scams vary, they all share common elements that make them effective. Understanding these mechanics can provide deeper insights into how scams operate and how to defend against them.

One key element is **social engineering**, which involves manipulating people into performing actions or divulging confidential information. Social engineering exploits basic human traits, such as trust, fear, greed, and the desire to help others. Scammers craft their messages and scenarios to evoke these emotions, making it easier to bypass the victim's rational defenses.

Manipulation of context and environment is another critical factor. Scammers often create a sense of urgency or scarcity to pressure victims into making quick decisions. For example, a phishing email might claim that the recipient's account will be locked if they do not act immediately, while a bait and switch advertisement might state that the deal is only available for a limited time. By controlling the context in which the victim makes decisions, scammers increase the likelihood of compliance.

Exploitation of authority and credibility is also common in scams. By impersonating trusted figures or organizations, scammers leverage the existing credibility of these entities to gain the victim's trust. This is particularly effective in impersonation scams, where the scammer pretends to be someone the victim already knows and trusts.

Technical deception involves using technology to create convincing fake environments. In phishing and bait and switch scams, this might include creating counterfeit websites that closely mimic legitimate ones. In tech support scams, it could involve displaying fake error messages or system warnings on the victim's computer. The use of technology enhances the realism of the scam, making it more difficult for victims to distinguish between legitimate and fraudulent interactions.

Isolation and secrecy are tactics used to prevent victims from seeking advice or verifying the scam. Scammers often stress the importance of keeping the interaction confidential or create scenarios that isolate the victim from others who might offer support. For example, in CEO fraud, the scammer might instruct the victim not to discuss the transaction with anyone else in the company. By isolating the victim, scammers reduce the chances of their deception being uncovered.

Case Studies: Illustrating Common Scamming Techniques

Examining real-world case studies can provide valuable insights into how these scamming techniques are applied and the impact they have on victims.

One notable case is the **Target data breach** in 2013, which involved a sophisticated phishing attack. The attackers sent phishing emails to Target's third-party HVAC vendor, successfully compromising their network. Once inside, the attackers were able to access Target's point-of-sale system, stealing the credit card information of over 40 million customers. This case highlights the potential for phishing to have far-reaching consequences, affecting not just individuals but entire organizations and their customers.

Another example is the **Ashley Madison hack** in 2015, where the data of millions of users of the dating site was compromised. Following the breach, scammers used the stolen information to launch phishing campaigns and extortion attempts, threatening to expose users' private information unless they paid a ransom. This case demonstrates the interplay between data breaches and phishing, where compromised information is used to perpetrate further scams.

The **Fyre Festival** debacle in 2017 is a prime example of a bait and switch scam on a massive scale. The festival was promoted as a luxury music experience on a private island, with top-tier entertainment and accommodations. Attendees paid thousands of dollars for tickets, expecting a high-end event. However, upon arrival, they found substandard conditions, inadequate food, and a lack of basic amenities. The organizers had used the allure of a luxury event (the bait) to attract attendees, only to deliver a much inferior experience (the switch). This case underscores the importance of verifying claims and being cautious of offers that seem too good to be true.

The **Theranos scandal** is another illustrative case of impersonation and deception. Elizabeth Holmes, the founder of Theranos, falsely claimed that the company had developed revolutionary blood-testing technology. She secured investments and partnerships by impersonating a credible and trustworthy leader, backed by endorsements from high-profile individuals and organizations. When the truth emerged that the technology did not work as claimed, investors and patients suffered significant financial and emotional harm. This case highlights how the exploitation of authority and credibility can lead to widespread deception and damage.

Building Awareness and Resilience

Understanding common scamming techniques is the first step in building resilience against them. Awareness of how phishing, bait and switch, and impersonation scams operate enables individuals to recognize the signs of these scams and take proactive measures to protect themselves.

Education and training are essential components of scam prevention. Regularly updating oneself on the latest scam tactics and sharing this knowledge with others can create a more informed and vigilant community. Businesses can implement training programs for employees to help them identify and respond to phishing attempts and other scams. Schools and educational institutions can incorporate lessons on digital literacy and online safety into their curricula, equipping students with the skills to navigate the digital world securely.

Implementing strong security practices can also mitigate the risk of falling victim to scams. Using complex, unique passwords for different accounts, enabling multi-factor authentication, and regularly updating software can enhance online security. Monitoring financial accounts and credit reports for unusual activity can help detect and respond to potential fraud quickly.

Verifying the legitimacy of requests and offers is a critical step in avoiding scams. This involves independently confirming the identity of the requester or the authenticity of the offer through official channels. For example, if you receive a suspicious email from your bank, contact the bank directly using a known phone number or email address to verify the request. Avoiding the use of contact information provided in the suspicious message can prevent falling into a scammer's trap.

Being cautious of unsolicited communications is also important. Scammers often initiate contact through unexpected emails, phone calls, or messages. Treating unsolicited requests for personal information or money with skepticism and verifying their authenticity can help prevent falling victim to scams. Additionally, avoiding clicking on links or downloading attachments from unknown sources can reduce the risk of phishing and malware infections.

Maintaining a healthy skepticism of offers that seem too good to be true is crucial. Scammers often use attractive deals, high returns on investments, or exclusive opportunities to lure victims. Approaching such offers with caution and conducting thorough research before making any commitments can help identify potential scams.

Creating a supportive network of friends, family, and colleagues can provide additional protection against scams. Discussing suspicious offers or requests with trusted individuals can offer different perspectives and help identify potential red flags. Encouraging open communication and seeking advice from others can reduce the chances of falling victim to scams.

Institutional and Community Efforts

While individual actions are vital, institutional and community efforts play a significant role in combating scams. Organizations, businesses, and government agencies can implement measures to protect their clients and contribute to broader scam prevention efforts.

Businesses can enhance their security measures and educate their customers about common scams. Providing clear communication about company policies, such as never requesting personal information via email or phone, can help customers recognize fraudulent attempts. Offering resources and tools for customers to secure their accounts, such as transaction alerts and fraud detection services, can enhance protection.

Financial institutions are on the front lines of scam prevention. Banks and credit card companies can monitor for unusual account activity and alert customers to potential fraud. Offering resources and tools for customers to secure their accounts, such as transaction alerts and fraud detection services, can enhance protection. Financial institutions can also collaborate with law enforcement to identify and shut down fraudulent operations.

Government agencies have a crucial role in regulating and enforcing laws against scams. Establishing and enforcing consumer protection laws, investigating fraud, and prosecuting scammers are essential functions. Government agencies can also lead public awareness campaigns, providing information on how to recognize and report scams. Collaboration with international agencies is important in addressing cross-border scams and enhancing global efforts to combat fraud.

Public awareness and education campaigns can reach a wide audience, providing valuable information on how to recognize and avoid scams. Government agencies, consumer protection organizations, and community groups can collaborate to raise awareness through media, social networks, and community events. These campaigns can highlight current scam trends, provide tips for recognizing red flags, and encourage individuals to report suspicious activities.

International collaboration is increasingly important in combating scams that cross national borders. Scammers often operate in multiple countries, making it challenging for individual nations to address the issue effectively. International cooperation, including information sharing, joint investigations, and coordinated enforcement actions, can enhance global efforts to combat fraud.

Future Trends and Challenges

As technology and society continue to evolve, so do the tactics and methods of scammers. Anticipating future trends in scams can help individuals and institutions stay ahead of emerging threats and develop effective prevention strategies.

Artificial Intelligence (AI) and machine learning are likely to be leveraged by scammers to create more sophisticated and convincing scams. AI can analyze vast amounts of data to personalize scam messages, making them more relevant and believable to each target. Deepfake technology, which creates realistic but fake audio and video, can be used to impersonate trusted individuals, adding another layer of deception.

Cybersecurity advancements will continue to play a crucial role in scam prevention. Developing and deploying advanced security technologies, such as biometric authentication and blockchain, can enhance protection against fraud. However, as cybersecurity measures become more sophisticated, scammers will also adapt, necessitating ongoing vigilance and innovation.

Global collaboration in fighting scams will become increasingly important. Scammers often operate across borders, making it challenging for individual countries to address the issue effectively. International cooperation, including information sharing, joint investigations, and coordinated enforcement actions, will be essential in combating global scams.

Public awareness and education will remain foundational in scam prevention. As new scams emerge, continuous efforts to educate the public about these threats and how to avoid them will be necessary. Leveraging digital platforms and social media to reach a wide audience can enhance the effectiveness of awareness campaigns.

Common scamming techniques such as phishing, bait and switch, and impersonation rely on manipulating human psychology and exploiting technological vulnerabilities. By understanding these techniques and the psychological principles behind them, individuals can better protect themselves and their personal information. Building awareness, adopting strong security practices, and verifying the legitimacy of requests and offers are essential components of scam prevention.

Institutions and community efforts play a crucial role in protecting individuals from scams. Businesses, financial institutions, and government agencies must implement robust security measures, educate their customers, and enforce consumer protection laws. Anticipating future trends in scams and adapting prevention strategies accordingly will be crucial in maintaining security in an ever-evolving landscape.

Combating scams requires a collective effort. By fostering a culture of awareness, vigilance, and resilience, we can reduce the prevalence and impact of scams, protecting individuals and communities from the harmful consequences of fraud.

CHAPTER 2
RECOGNIZING
RED FLAGS

Recognizing red flags is crucial for protecting oneself from scams. Scammers often use psychological manipulation and create deceptive situations to exploit their victims' vulnerabilities. By understanding and identifying common warning signs, individuals can better guard against fraudulent schemes. This chapter explores several key red flags, including offers that seem too good to be true, urgency and pressure tactics, and unusual payment methods, providing detailed insights into how these tactics work and how to avoid falling victim to them.

Too Good to Be True

One of the most common red flags indicating a scam is an offer that seems too good to be true. Scammers use enticing promises of extraordinary benefits to lure victims. These offers often include substantial financial rewards, free products, or exclusive opportunities that are unrealistic or improbable. Understanding how this tactic works can help individuals recognize and avoid falling prey to such scams.

Scammers are adept at crafting messages that tap into the natural human desire for wealth, success, and happiness. For example, a common scam involves sending an email or message claiming that the recipient has won a large sum of money in a lottery or sweepstakes. The message might state that the recipient was randomly selected from a pool of participants and is now eligible to claim a prize worth millions of dollars. The scammer typically asks for personal information or a small fee to process the claim. The allure of easy money can cloud the victim's judgment, leading them to overlook the improbability of winning a lottery they never entered.

Another example is the investment scam, where scammers promise high returns with little or no risk. These schemes often involve enticing narratives about groundbreaking technologies, exclusive opportunities, or insider information. For instance, a scammer might promote an investment in a new cryptocurrency, claiming that it is poised to revolutionize the market and generate massive profits. The scammer may provide fake testimonials and doctored financial statements to create the illusion of legitimacy. Victims, driven by the desire to capitalize on the opportunity, may invest significant sums of money, only to discover that the investment was a fraud.

In the realm of online shopping, too-good-to-be-true offers often involve counterfeit or non-existent products. Scammers set up fake websites or use online marketplaces to advertise popular items, such as electronics, fashion items, or luxury goods, at significantly reduced prices. The victim, attracted by the bargain, makes a purchase, only to receive a substandard product or nothing at all. The scammer may also steal the victim's payment information for further fraudulent activities.

To recognize and avoid offers that are too good to be true, individuals should adopt a healthy dose of skepticism. Critical thinking and due diligence are essential in evaluating the legitimacy of such offers. Here are some strategies to help identify and avoid these scams:

1. **Research the Offer**: Before responding to any offer, take the time to research it thoroughly. Look for reviews and testimonials from independent sources.

If the offer involves a company or product, check for its legitimacy through official websites and consumer protection agencies. Verify the credentials of the individuals or organizations promoting the offer.

2. **Check for Red Flags**: Be on the lookout for common warning signs, such as unsolicited messages, generic greetings, and poor grammar or spelling. Scammers often use these tactics to cast a wide net, hoping to catch unsuspecting victims.

3. **Verify the Source**: If the offer claims to be from a reputable organization, contact the organization directly using official contact details. Do not use the contact information provided in the suspicious message. Verify the legitimacy of the offer through official channels.

4. **Beware of Upfront Fees**: Be cautious of offers that require upfront payments or personal information. Legitimate organizations typically do not ask for fees to claim prizes or process transactions. If an offer requires you to pay money or provide sensitive information, it is likely a scam.

5. **Trust Your Instincts**: If something feels off or too good to be true, trust your instincts. Scammers rely on creating a sense of urgency and excitement to bypass rational judgment. Taking a step back and evaluating the offer critically can help you avoid falling victim to a scam.

Urgency and Pressure

Another common tactic used by scammers is creating a sense of urgency and pressure. By convincing victims that immediate action is required, scammers can override their natural caution and prompt them to make hasty decisions. Understanding how urgency and pressure are used in scams can help individuals recognize and resist these manipulative tactics.

Scammers often create scenarios that evoke fear, excitement, or the fear of missing out (FOMO). These emotions can cloud judgment and lead individuals to act impulsively. For example, a scammer might send an email claiming that the recipient's bank account has been compromised and immediate action is required to prevent unauthorized transactions. The email may include urgent language, such as "act now" or "immediate response required," to create a sense of panic. The victim, fearing financial loss, may follow the instructions without verifying the authenticity of the message.

In another example, scammers use urgency in phishing schemes. An email might appear to come from a well-known online retailer, stating that the recipient's recent order cannot be processed due to a problem with their payment information. The email urges the recipient to click on a link and update their information immediately to avoid delays in shipping. The fear of not receiving a purchased item can prompt the victim to act quickly, providing their payment details to the scammer.

Urgency and pressure are also commonly used in lottery and prize scams. The scammer might send a message claiming that the recipient has won a significant prize but must claim it within a limited timeframe. The message may state that if the recipient does not respond quickly, they will forfeit the prize. The fear of losing out on a valuable reward can lead the victim to provide personal information or pay a fee to claim the non-existent prize.

Romance scams often use urgency and pressure to manipulate victims emotionally. After establishing a relationship and gaining the victim's trust, the scammer fabricates a crisis that requires immediate financial assistance. For example, the scammer might claim to be stranded in a foreign country without access to funds, facing a medical emergency, or needing money for urgent travel expenses. The victim, driven by concern and affection, may send money quickly, without considering the possibility of deception.

Investment scams frequently use high-pressure sales tactics to create a sense of urgency. Scammers might present an investment opportunity with the promise of exceptional returns but stress that the opportunity is available for a limited time only. They may use phrases like "limited slots available," "act fast," or "once-in-a-lifetime opportunity" to push the victim into making a quick decision. The fear of missing out on a lucrative investment can override the victim's critical thinking, leading them to invest without proper research.

To recognize and resist urgency and pressure tactics, individuals should adopt a measured and deliberate approach to decision-making. Here are some strategies to help avoid falling victim to these scams:

1. **Take Your Time**: Do not let anyone rush you into making a decision. Scammers rely on creating a sense of urgency to bypass your natural caution. Take the time to evaluate the situation, verify the information, and consider your options before taking any action.

2. **Verify the Source**: If you receive an urgent request for personal information or payment, verify the authenticity of the request through independent channels. Contact the organization or individual directly using known contact details, rather than those provided in the suspicious message.

3. **Ask Questions**: If something feels urgent, ask questions to gather more information. Scammers often struggle to provide consistent and detailed answers. Asking for specifics can help you identify inconsistencies and recognize a potential scam.

4. **Consult Trusted Individuals**: Discuss the situation with trusted friends, family members, or colleagues.

They can offer a different perspective and help you evaluate the legitimacy of the request. Scammers often rely on isolating their victims, so seeking input from others can disrupt their tactics.

5. **Trust Your Instincts**: If something feels off or too urgent, trust your instincts. High-pressure tactics are a red flag, and taking a step back to assess the situation can help you avoid making impulsive decisions.

Unusual Payment Methods

Scammers frequently request payment through unusual methods that make it difficult to trace or recover the funds. Recognizing these red flags can help individuals avoid falling victim to financial scams. Understanding how scammers use these payment methods and why they prefer them can provide valuable insights into identifying and avoiding fraudulent schemes.

One common payment method used by scammers is the **wire transfer**. Wire transfers are popular among scammers because they are fast, irreversible, and difficult to trace. Once the victim sends the money, it is nearly impossible to get it back. Scammers often ask for wire transfers in scenarios such as advance-fee fraud, lottery and prize scams, and romance scams. For example, in a romance scam, the scammer might build a relationship with the victim and then fabricate a crisis that requires immediate financial assistance.

The scammer asks the victim to wire money to help resolve the situation, knowing that once the money is sent, it cannot be recovered.

Another unusual payment method favored by scammers is the use of **gift cards**. Scammers instruct victims to purchase gift cards and provide the card numbers and PINs. This method is appealing to scammers because gift cards are essentially cash equivalents and can be used or sold easily.

Scammers might claim that the victim needs to pay a fee or tax to claim a prize or that they need to settle a debt or avoid legal action. By requesting payment in gift cards, scammers make it difficult for authorities to trace the transaction and recover the funds.

Cryptocurrency has become an increasingly popular payment method for scammers due to its anonymity and irreversibility. Scammers might ask victims to send payments in Bitcoin, Ethereum, or other cryptocurrencies, making it challenging to trace the transactions and identify the recipients. Cryptocurrency scams can take various forms, including investment scams, ransomware attacks, and online marketplace fraud. For example, in an investment scam, the scammer might promote a new cryptocurrency or investment platform, promising high returns. The victim is asked to transfer their funds into a cryptocurrency wallet, only to discover that the investment was a fraud and their money is gone.

Prepaid debit cards are another method used by scammers. Similar to gift cards, prepaid debit cards are difficult to trace and provide a convenient way for scammers to access cash. Victims might be instructed to purchase prepaid debit cards and provide the card information to the scammer. This method is often used in tech support scams, where the scammer claims to be fixing a problem on the victim's computer and requires payment in prepaid debit cards.

Payment apps and **peer-to-peer (P2P) payment services**, such as Venmo, Cash App, and Zelle, are also used by scammers. These apps offer convenience and speed, but once a payment is sent, it is challenging to reverse. Scammers might ask for payment through these apps, claiming it is a quick and secure method. For example, in an online marketplace scam, the scammer might sell a product at a low price and ask for payment through a P2P service. Once the victim sends the payment, the scammer disappears, and the victim receives nothing in return.

To recognize and avoid scams involving unusual payment methods, individuals should be cautious when asked to use non-traditional payment methods. Here are some strategies to help identify and avoid these scams:

1. **Understand Legitimate Payment Methods**: Familiarize yourself with the standard payment methods used by reputable businesses and organizations. Legitimate companies typically accept credit cards, checks, and other traceable payment methods. Be wary of any request for payment through wire transfers, gift cards, cryptocurrency, or prepaid debit cards.

2. **Verify Payment Requests**: If you receive a request for payment through an unusual method, verify the legitimacy of the request independently. Contact the organization or individual directly using known contact details and confirm that the payment request is legitimate.

3. **Avoid Pressure to Use Unusual Methods**: Scammers often pressure victims to use unusual payment methods by creating a sense of urgency. Resist the pressure and take the time to verify the request. Legitimate organizations will not rush you into making a payment through an unconventional method.

4. **Report Suspicious Requests**: If you encounter a suspicious payment request, report it to the relevant authorities or consumer protection agencies. Reporting scams can help prevent others from falling

victim and assist in efforts to identify and apprehend scammers.

5. **Educate Yourself and Others**: Stay informed about common scamming tactics and unusual payment methods. Share this knowledge with friends, family members, and colleagues to help them recognize and avoid scams.

Case Studies: Illustrating Red Flags

Examining real-world case studies can provide valuable insights into how scammers use red flags such as too-good-to-be-true offers, urgency and pressure, and unusual payment methods to deceive their victims. These examples highlight the importance of recognizing and responding to these red flags to protect oneself from fraud.

One notable case involves the infamous **Nigerian Prince** scam, also known as the 419 scam. In this scam, victims receive an email from someone claiming to be a Nigerian prince or government official who needs help transferring a large sum of money out of the country. The email promises the victim a substantial reward for their assistance but requires an upfront payment to cover administrative fees or taxes. The too-good-to-be-true offer of a significant financial reward, combined with the urgency to act quickly, lures victims into sending money. Despite the improbability of the scenario, the allure of easy money and the pressure to comply lead many victims to fall for the scam.

Another example is the **IRS imposter scam**, where scammers pose as IRS agents and contact victims by phone, claiming that they owe back taxes and must pay immediately to avoid arrest or legal action. The scammers use urgency and fear to pressure victims into making quick decisions. They often demand payment through unusual methods, such as wire transfers or prepaid debit cards, making it difficult to trace the transactions.

Victims, fearing the consequences of not complying, may follow the scammers' instructions and lose significant amounts of money.

In the **grandparent scam**, scammers target elderly individuals by posing as their grandchildren in distress. The scammer contacts the victim, claiming to be in a foreign country and needing money for bail, medical expenses, or other emergencies. The urgency and emotional manipulation, combined with the unusual payment method of wire transfers or gift cards, create a convincing scenario that leads the victim to send money without verifying the legitimacy of the request. The victim, driven by concern for their loved one, acts quickly to provide assistance, only to discover that the entire situation was fabricated.

The **romance scam** is another illustrative case, where scammers create fake profiles on dating sites or social media platforms to build relationships with victims. After gaining the victim's trust, the scammer fabricates a crisis that requires immediate financial assistance, such as a medical emergency or travel expenses. The sense of urgency and emotional manipulation, combined with requests for wire transfers or cryptocurrency payments, lead victims to send money without realizing they are being deceived. The emotional investment and the fear of losing a loved one drive the victim to comply with the scammer's demands.

In the **fake tech support scam**, victims receive unsolicited calls from scammers posing as technical support representatives from well-known companies like Microsoft or Apple. The scammer claims that the victim's computer is infected with a virus or has a technical issue that needs immediate attention. The urgency and fear created by the supposed threat to the victim's computer, combined with the unusual payment method of prepaid debit cards or gift cards, prompt the victim to follow the scammer's instructions. The scammer gains remote access to the victim's computer, steals personal information, or demands payment for unnecessary services.

Building Awareness and Resilience

Recognizing red flags is essential in building awareness and resilience against scams. By understanding how too-good-to-be-true offers, urgency and pressure, and unusual payment methods are used by scammers, individuals can better protect themselves and others. Here are some strategies to build awareness and resilience:

1. **Stay Informed**: Regularly update yourself on the latest scam tactics and red flags. Consumer protection agencies, news outlets, and online resources provide valuable information on emerging scams and how to avoid them.

2. **Educate Others**: Share your knowledge with friends, family members, and colleagues. Raising awareness within your community can help others recognize and avoid scams. Encourage open discussions about suspicious offers and requests.

3. **Develop Critical Thinking Skills**: Practice critical thinking and skepticism when evaluating offers and requests. Question the legitimacy of too-good-to-be-true offers, verify the authenticity of urgent requests, and be cautious of unusual payment methods.

4. **Create a Support Network**: Build a support network of trusted individuals with whom you can discuss suspicious situations. Consulting others can provide different perspectives and help identify potential red flags.

5. **Implement Security Measures**: Use robust security measures to protect your personal information and financial accounts. This includes using strong, unique passwords, enabling multi-factor authentication, and

regularly monitoring your accounts for unusual activity.

6. **Report Scams**: If you encounter a scam or suspicious request, report it to the relevant authorities or consumer protection agencies. Reporting scams helps prevent others from falling victim and contributes to efforts to combat fraud.

Institutional and Community Efforts

While individual actions are crucial, institutional and community efforts play a significant role in recognizing and addressing red flags in scams. Organizations, businesses, and government agencies can implement measures to protect individuals and contribute to broader scam prevention efforts.

Businesses can enhance their security practices and educate their customers about common scam tactics. Providing clear communication about company policies, such as never requesting personal information or payments through unusual methods, can help customers recognize fraudulent attempts. Offering resources and tools for customers to secure their accounts, such as transaction alerts and fraud detection services, can enhance protection.

Financial institutions are on the front lines of scam prevention. Banks and credit card companies can monitor for unusual account activity and alert customers to potential fraud. Offering resources and tools for customers to secure their accounts, such as transaction alerts and fraud detection services, can enhance protection. Financial institutions can also collaborate with law enforcement to identify and shut down fraudulent operations.

Government agencies have a crucial role in regulating and enforcing laws against scams. Establishing and enforcing consumer protection laws, investigating fraud, and prosecuting scammers are essential functions. Government agencies can also lead public awareness campaigns, providing information on how to recognize and report scams. Collaboration with international agencies is important in addressing cross-border scams and enhancing global efforts to combat fraud.

Public awareness and education campaigns can reach a wide audience, providing valuable information on how to recognize and avoid scams. Government agencies, consumer protection organizations, and community groups can collaborate to raise awareness through media, social networks, and community events. These campaigns can highlight current scam trends, provide tips for recognizing red flags, and encourage individuals to report suspicious activities.

International collaboration is increasingly important in combating scams that cross national borders. Scammers often operate in multiple countries, making it challenging for individual nations to address the issue effectively. International cooperation, including information sharing, joint investigations, and coordinated enforcement actions, can enhance global efforts to combat fraud.

Future Trends and Challenges

As technology and society continue to evolve, so do the tactics and methods of scammers. Anticipating future trends in scams can help individuals and institutions stay ahead of emerging threats and develop effective prevention strategies.

Artificial Intelligence (AI) and machine learning are likely to be leveraged by scammers to create more sophisticated and convincing scams. AI can analyze vast amounts of data to personalize scam messages, making them more relevant and believable to each target. Deepfake technology, which creates realistic but fake audio and video, can be used to impersonate trusted individuals, adding another layer of deception.

Cybersecurity advancements will continue to play a crucial role in scam prevention. Developing and deploying advanced security technologies, such as biometric authentication and blockchain, can enhance protection against fraud. However, as cybersecurity measures become more sophisticated, scammers will also adapt, necessitating ongoing vigilance and innovation.

Global collaboration in fighting scams will become increasingly important. Scammers often operate across borders, making it challenging for individual countries to address the issue effectively. International cooperation, including information sharing, joint investigations, and coordinated enforcement actions, will be essential in combating global scams.

Public awareness and education will remain foundational in scam prevention. As new scams emerge, continuous efforts to educate the public about these threats and how to avoid them will be necessary. Leveraging digital platforms and social media to reach a wide audience can enhance the effectiveness of awareness campaigns.

Recognizing red flags such as too-good-to-be-true offers, urgency and pressure, and unusual payment methods is essential in protecting oneself from scams. By understanding how these tactics are used by scammers, individuals can build awareness and resilience, making it more difficult for scammers to succeed.

Individual actions, such as staying informed, educating others, developing critical thinking skills, and implementing security measures, are crucial in recognizing and responding to red flags. Institutional and community efforts, including public awareness campaigns, consumer protection laws, and international collaboration, play a significant role in creating a safer environment.

Anticipating future trends and challenges in scam tactics can help individuals and institutions stay ahead of emerging threats. By fostering a culture of awareness, vigilance, and resilience, we can reduce the prevalence and impact of scams, protecting individuals and communities from the harmful consequences of fraud.

CHAPTER 3 REAL-LIFE EXAMPLES

Understanding scams through real-life examples provides valuable insights into how these fraudulent schemes operate and the impact they have on victims. By examining detailed stories of common scams, analyzing what went wrong, and exploring how these situations could have been avoided, we can better equip ourselves to recognize and prevent similar incidents. This chapter delves into several case studies, offering a comprehensive look at the mechanics of scams and the lessons they impart.

Case Study: The Nigerian Prince Scam

The Nigerian Prince scam, also known as the 419 scam, is one of the most infamous and enduring types of fraud. It typically begins with an unsolicited email from someone claiming to be a wealthy individual or government official from Nigeria (or another country) who needs help transferring a large sum of money out of their country. In return for the victim's assistance, the scammer promises a substantial reward.

One notable case involved a man named John, who received an email from "Prince Adebayo," claiming to be the son of a deposed Nigerian king. Prince Adebayo explained that he had $20 million that he needed to transfer to a safe account in the United States, and he offered John 20% of the total amount for his help. The email seemed convincing, with official-looking letterhead and a compelling story.

John, enticed by the prospect of easy money, responded to the email. The scammer then requested that John provide his bank account details to facilitate the transfer. As the correspondence continued, Prince Adebayo claimed that various administrative fees, taxes, and legal expenses needed to be paid before the transfer could be completed. Over several weeks, John wired multiple payments, totaling over $10,000, to various accounts specified by the scammer.

Eventually, John realized that the promised $20 million was never going to materialize, and he reported the scam to the authorities. Unfortunately, the chances of recovering his money were slim, as the transactions had been sent to multiple international accounts.

Analysis:

- **What Went Wrong:** John fell victim to a classic advance-fee scam, driven by the allure of easy money. He failed to verify the legitimacy of the email and its sender, instead trusting the well-crafted narrative.

- **How It Could Have Been Avoided:** John could have avoided this scam by recognizing the red flags associated with too-good-to-be-true offers. Conducting a quick online search about Nigerian Prince scams would have revealed numerous warnings about this type of fraud. Additionally, consulting with friends, family, or financial advisors before making any payments could have provided critical perspective and caution.

Case Study: The IRS Imposter Scam

In the IRS imposter scam, fraudsters pose as IRS agents and contact victims, claiming that they owe back taxes and must pay immediately to avoid arrest or other severe consequences. This scam exploits fear and urgency to pressure victims into complying with the demands.

Emily, a small business owner, received a phone call from someone claiming to be an IRS agent. The caller, who spoke with authority and used IRS jargon, informed Emily that she owed $5,000 in back taxes and that a warrant for her arrest would be issued if she did not pay immediately. The caller instructed Emily to stay on the line and drive to the nearest store to purchase prepaid debit cards to cover the amount.

Panicked and fearing legal trouble, Emily followed the instructions. She purchased the prepaid debit cards and provided the card numbers and PINs to the caller. After hanging up, Emily felt uneasy and decided to contact the IRS directly. She soon learned that the call was a scam and that the IRS would never demand payment in such a manner.

Analysis:

- **What Went Wrong:** Emily was manipulated by the scammer's use of fear and urgency. She did not verify the authenticity of the call and acted quickly under pressure.

- **How It Could Have Been Avoided:** Emily could have avoided this scam by taking a moment to verify the caller's identity. The IRS typically communicates through official letters, not phone calls demanding immediate payment. Consulting the IRS website or calling the official IRS hotline could have provided clarity and prevented the scam. Additionally, being aware of common scam tactics, such as demands for payment via prepaid debit cards, could have raised red flags.

Case Study: The Grandparent Scam

The grandparent scam targets elderly individuals by exploiting their love and concern for their family members. Scammers pose as grandchildren in distress and request urgent financial assistance.

Margaret, an 82-year-old grandmother, received a frantic phone call from someone claiming to be her grandson, Jack. The caller explained that he had been in a car accident while traveling abroad and needed money to pay for medical expenses and legal fees. The caller pleaded with Margaret not to tell his parents, as he was embarrassed and didn't want them to worry.

Concerned for her grandson's well-being, Margaret agreed to help. The caller instructed her to wire $2,000 to a foreign account. Margaret did as instructed, believing she was assisting her grandson in a time of need. It wasn't until she mentioned the situation to her daughter later that day that she realized she had been scammed. Her daughter immediately called Jack, who was safe at home and unaware of the situation.

Analysis:

- **What Went Wrong:** Margaret's emotional response to the plea for help clouded her judgment. She did not verify the caller's identity or discuss the situation with other family members before taking action.

- **How It Could Have Been Avoided:** Margaret could have avoided this scam by asking the caller questions that only her real grandson would know the answers to. Additionally, she could have verified the situation by contacting her grandson or his parents directly.

Scammers often rely on secrecy and urgency, so discussing the situation with trusted family members could have provided clarity and prevented the scam.

Case Study: The Romance Scam

Romance scams involve scammers creating fake profiles on dating sites or social media platforms to build relationships with victims. Once trust and affection are established, the scammer fabricates a crisis and requests financial assistance.

Linda, a 45-year-old divorcee, met "James" on a popular dating site. James claimed to be a successful businessman working on an international project. Over several months, Linda and James exchanged messages, phone calls, and video chats (where James used pre-recorded videos). They developed a deep emotional connection, and Linda believed she had found true love.

One day, James told Linda that he was in a foreign country for a business deal, and things had gone wrong. He claimed his bank accounts were frozen due to a legal dispute, and he needed $10,000 to resolve the issue and return home. Concerned for James's safety and wanting to help, Linda wired the money to the account he provided.

Weeks passed, and James's situation seemed to worsen. He requested more money for various emergencies, and Linda complied, ultimately sending over $50,000. When James's communication became sporadic, Linda grew suspicious and contacted the dating site. She discovered that James's profile had been flagged for fraudulent activity and that she had been scammed.

Analysis:

- **What Went Wrong:** Linda was manipulated by the emotional connection she had developed with James.

She did not verify his identity or question the plausibility of his crises.

- **How It Could Have Been Avoided:** Linda could have avoided this scam by conducting a reverse image search of James's profile pictures, which might have revealed their use on multiple scam profiles. Additionally, discussing the situation with friends or family members could have provided a reality check. Being aware of common red flags in online dating, such as requests for money, could have helped Linda recognize the scam.

Case Study: The Fake Tech Support Scam

Tech support scams involve scammers posing as technical support representatives from well-known companies. They claim that the victim's computer is infected with a virus or has a technical issue that needs immediate attention, often requesting remote access to the computer or payment for unnecessary services.

Tom, a 60-year-old retiree, received a pop-up message on his computer claiming that his system was infected with malware and that he needed to call Microsoft support immediately. The message included a phone number and warned of severe consequences if he did not act quickly.

Frightened by the warning, Tom called the number and spoke with "Steve," who claimed to be a Microsoft technician. Steve instructed Tom to download and install a remote access tool, which allowed Steve to control Tom's computer. Steve then showed Tom a series of fake error messages and claimed that his computer was severely compromised.

Steve offered to fix the issues for a fee of $300, payable via gift cards. Desperate to resolve the problem, Tom purchased the gift cards and provided the card numbers to Steve. After "fixing" the computer, Steve disappeared, and Tom realized that his computer was still experiencing issues. He later learned that he had been scammed and that the pop-up message was a fake alert designed to trick him.

Analysis:

- **What Went Wrong:** Tom was manipulated by the fear of his computer being infected and trusted the fake tech support representative. He did not verify the legitimacy of the pop-up message or the support call.

- **How It Could Have Been Avoided:** Tom could have avoided this scam by recognizing that legitimate tech companies do not send unsolicited pop-up messages or request payment via gift cards. Verifying the issue through official channels, such as contacting Microsoft support directly using known contact details, could have prevented the scam. Additionally, being aware of common tech support scam tactics could have helped Tom identify the red flags.

Case Study: The Investment Scam

Investment scams entice victims with the promise of high returns with little or no risk. These scams often involve fake investment opportunities, Ponzi schemes, or fraudulent financial advisors.

Michael, an aspiring investor, was introduced to an investment opportunity by "David," who claimed to be a financial advisor with a track record of delivering exceptional returns. David presented a detailed investment plan, complete with fake financial statements and glowing testimonials from supposed clients.

Impressed by the potential for significant profits, Michael invested $20,000 in the scheme. Over the next few months, David provided regular updates, showing impressive gains on the investment. Encouraged by the apparent success, Michael invested an additional $30,000.

However, when Michael attempted to withdraw some of his profits, David became evasive and made various excuses to delay the payout. Eventually, David stopped responding to Michael's calls and emails. Michael realized that he had been scammed and that the investment was a fraud.

Analysis:

- **What Went Wrong:** Michael was deceived by the convincing presentation and testimonials. He did not conduct thorough due diligence on the investment or verify David's credentials.

- **How It Could Have Been Avoided:** Michael could have avoided this scam by researching David's background and checking for any regulatory registrations or licenses. Consulting with an independent financial advisor or conducting a background check on the investment opportunity could have revealed red flags. Being wary of promises of high returns with little risk and seeking advice from trusted sources could have provided additional protection.

Case Study: The Rental Scam

Rental scams involve scammers advertising properties for rent that they do not own or that do not exist. They typically request upfront payments for deposits or rent before the victim has seen the property.

Sarah, a college student, was searching for an apartment to rent near her university. She found a listing for a spacious apartment at a very reasonable price on a popular rental website. The listing included photos of a well-furnished apartment and a detailed description of the amenities.

Sarah contacted the "landlord," who claimed to be out of the country on business but assured her that the apartment was available. The landlord requested that Sarah wire the first month's rent and a security deposit to secure the rental, promising to send the keys by mail.

Eager to secure the apartment, Sarah sent the money as instructed. However, after the payment was made, the landlord stopped responding to her messages. Sarah never received the keys, and when she visited the address, she found that the apartment was already occupied and not available for rent. Realizing she had been scammed, Sarah reported the incident to the rental website and the authorities.

Analysis:

- **What Went Wrong:** Sarah was deceived by the appealing listing and the urgency to secure the rental. She did not verify the legitimacy of the landlord or the property before making the payment.

- **How It Could Have Been Avoided:** Sarah could have avoided this scam by insisting on meeting the landlord in person or working with a reputable rental agency. Verifying the property through a visit or requesting to speak with current tenants could have provided assurance. Being cautious of requests for wire transfers and researching the rental website's guidelines for avoiding scams could have helped identify the red flags.

Building Awareness and Resilience

Real-life examples of scams highlight the importance of awareness and resilience in protecting oneself from fraud. By understanding how these scams operate and recognizing common red flags, individuals can better equip themselves to avoid falling victim to similar schemes. Here are some strategies to build awareness and resilience:

1. **Stay Informed:** Regularly update yourself on the latest scam tactics and red flags. Consumer protection agencies, news outlets, and online resources provide valuable information on emerging scams and how to avoid them.

2. **Educate Others:** Share your knowledge with friends, family members, and colleagues. Raising awareness within your community can help others recognize and avoid scams. Encourage open discussions about suspicious offers and requests.

3. **Develop Critical Thinking Skills:** Practice critical thinking and skepticism when evaluating offers and requests. Question the legitimacy of too-good-to-be-true offers, verify the authenticity of urgent requests, and be cautious of unusual payment methods.

4. **Create a Support Network:** Build a support network of trusted individuals with whom you can discuss suspicious situations. Consulting others can provide different perspectives and help identify potential red flags.

5. **Implement Security Measures:** Use robust security measures to protect your personal information and financial accounts. This includes using strong, unique passwords, enabling multi-factor authentication, and regularly monitoring your accounts for unusual

activity.

6. **Report Scams:** If you encounter a scam or suspicious request, report it to the relevant authorities or consumer protection agencies. Reporting scams helps prevent others from falling victim and contributes to efforts to combat fraud.

Institutional and Community Efforts

While individual actions are crucial, institutional and community efforts play a significant role in recognizing and addressing scams. Organizations, businesses, and government agencies can implement measures to protect individuals and contribute to broader scam prevention efforts.

Businesses can enhance their security practices and educate their customers about common scam tactics. Providing clear communication about company policies, such as never requesting personal information or payments through unusual methods, can help customers recognize fraudulent attempts. Offering resources and tools for customers to secure their accounts, such as transaction alerts and fraud detection services, can enhance protection.

Financial institutions are on the front lines of scam prevention. Banks and credit card companies can monitor for unusual account activity and alert customers to potential fraud. Offering resources and tools for customers to secure their accounts, such as transaction alerts and fraud detection services, can enhance protection. Financial institutions can also collaborate with law enforcement to identify and shut down fraudulent operations.

Government agencies have a crucial role in regulating and enforcing laws against scams. Establishing and enforcing consumer protection laws, investigating fraud, and prosecuting scammers are essential functions. Government agencies can also lead public awareness campaigns, providing information on how to recognize and report scams. Collaboration with international agencies is important in addressing cross-border scams and enhancing global efforts to combat fraud.

Public awareness and education campaigns can reach a wide audience, providing valuable information on how to recognize and avoid scams. Government agencies, consumer protection organizations, and community groups can collaborate to raise awareness through media, social networks, and community events. These campaigns can highlight current scam trends, provide tips for recognizing red flags, and encourage individuals to report suspicious activities.

International collaboration is increasingly important in combating scams that cross national borders. Scammers often operate in multiple countries, making it challenging for individual nations to address the issue effectively. International cooperation, including information sharing, joint investigations, and coordinated enforcement actions, can enhance global efforts to combat fraud.

Future Trends and Challenges

As technology and society continue to evolve, so do the tactics and methods of scammers. Anticipating future trends in scams can help individuals and institutions stay ahead of emerging threats and develop effective prevention strategies.

Artificial Intelligence (AI) and machine learning are likely to be leveraged by scammers to create more sophisticated and convincing scams. AI can analyze vast amounts of data to personalize scam messages, making them more relevant and believable to each target. Deepfake technology, which creates realistic but fake audio and video, can be used to impersonate trusted individuals, adding another layer of deception.

Cybersecurity advancements will continue to play a crucial role in scam prevention. Developing and deploying advanced security technologies, such as biometric authentication and blockchain, can enhance protection against fraud. However, as cybersecurity measures become more sophisticated, scammers will also adapt, necessitating ongoing vigilance and innovation.

Global collaboration in fighting scams will become increasingly important. Scammers often operate across borders, making it challenging for individual countries to address the issue effectively. International cooperation, including information sharing, joint investigations, and coordinated enforcement actions, will be essential in combating global scams.

Public awareness and education will remain foundational in scam prevention. As new scams emerge, continuous efforts to educate the public about these threats and how to avoid them will be necessary. Leveraging digital platforms and social media to reach a wide audience can enhance the effectiveness of awareness campaigns.

Real-life examples of scams provide valuable insights into the tactics and methods used by fraudsters. By analyzing detailed stories of common scams, understanding what went wrong, and exploring how these situations could have been avoided, individuals can better equip themselves to recognize and prevent similar incidents.

Recognizing red flags, such as too-good-to-be-true offers, urgency and pressure, and unusual payment methods, is essential in protecting oneself from scams. Building awareness and resilience through education, critical thinking, and robust security measures can help individuals avoid falling victim to fraud.

Institutional and community efforts, including public awareness campaigns, consumer protection laws, and international collaboration, play a significant role in creating a safer environment. Anticipating future trends and challenges in scam tactics can help individuals and institutions stay ahead of emerging threats and develop effective prevention strategies.

By fostering a culture of awareness, vigilance, and resilience, we can reduce the prevalence and impact of scams, protecting individuals and communities from the harmful consequences of fraud.

CHAPTER 4
PROTECTING
YOURSELF ONLINE

In the digital age, protecting yourself online is more crucial than ever. The internet offers vast opportunities for communication, commerce, and entertainment, but it also presents significant risks. Cybercriminals are continually devising new methods to exploit vulnerabilities and deceive unsuspecting users. To safeguard yourself against these threats, it is essential to adopt safe internet practices, secure your browsing habits, recognize phishing emails, be aware of social media risks, protect your personal information, spot fake profiles, ensure secure transactions, make safe online purchases, and avoid fake websites.

Safe Internet Practices

Safe internet practices form the foundation of online security. By developing good habits and adhering to certain guidelines, you can significantly reduce your risk of falling victim to cyber threats.

One of the most fundamental safe internet practices is the use of strong, unique passwords for each of your online accounts. A strong password typically includes a combination of upper and lowercase letters, numbers, and special characters. Avoid using easily guessable information such as your name, birthdate, or common words. Password managers can help you generate and store complex passwords securely.

Regularly updating your software and devices is another critical practice. Software updates often include patches for security vulnerabilities that cybercriminals could exploit. Ensuring that your operating system, web browser, antivirus software, and other applications are up to date can provide an additional layer of protection.

Enabling multi-factor authentication (MFA) on your accounts adds an extra layer of security. MFA requires you to provide two or more verification factors to gain access to your account, such as a password and a code sent to your mobile device. This makes it much harder for cybercriminals to gain unauthorized access, even if they have your password.

Being cautious with email attachments and links is also essential. Cybercriminals often use email to distribute malware or direct victims to phishing websites. Avoid opening attachments or clicking on links from unknown or suspicious sources. Even if an email appears to be from a trusted contact, verify its authenticity if it seems out of character.

Regularly backing up your data can mitigate the impact of certain cyber threats, such as ransomware attacks. By maintaining secure copies of your important files, you can recover your data without having to pay a ransom if your system is compromised.

Secure Browsing

Secure browsing practices are crucial for protecting your online activities from cyber threats. One of the first steps in secure browsing is ensuring that you are using a reputable and up-to-date web browser. Modern browsers come with built-in security features that help protect against phishing, malware, and other threats.

When browsing the internet, always check for HTTPS in the URL before entering sensitive information. HTTPS indicates that the website uses encryption to secure the data transmitted between your browser and the website. A padlock icon in the address bar also signifies a secure connection. Be cautious of websites that only use HTTP, as they do not provide the same level of security.

Avoiding public Wi-Fi for sensitive activities is another important aspect of secure browsing. Public Wi-Fi networks, such as those found in coffee shops or airports, are often unsecured and can be exploited by cybercriminals to intercept your data. If you must use public Wi-Fi, consider using a virtual private network (VPN) to encrypt your internet traffic and protect your privacy.

Clearing your browser's cache and cookies regularly can help protect your privacy and reduce the risk of tracking. Browsers store information about your browsing history, login credentials, and preferences, which can be accessed by malicious actors if your device is compromised. Regularly clearing this data can limit the amount of information available to potential attackers.

Using browser extensions and add-ons designed to enhance security and privacy can also be beneficial. Tools such as ad blockers, anti-tracking extensions, and script blockers can help protect you from malicious ads, prevent tracking, and block potentially harmful scripts.

Recognizing Phishing Emails

Phishing emails are a common method used by cybercriminals to steal personal information, login credentials, and financial details. Recognizing the signs of a phishing email can help you avoid falling victim to these scams.

Phishing emails often create a sense of urgency or fear to prompt immediate action. For example, the email might claim that there has been suspicious activity on your account, and you need to verify your information immediately. Be cautious of emails that pressure you to act quickly without giving you time to verify their legitimacy.

Check the sender's email address carefully. Phishing emails often come from addresses that look similar to those of legitimate organizations but may have slight variations, such as extra characters or misspellings. For instance, an email from "security@yourbank.com" might be spoofed as "security@yourb4nk.com." If you receive an unexpected email from a familiar organization, it's best to contact them directly using known contact information rather than the details provided in the email.

Look for generic greetings and poor grammar. Legitimate organizations typically address you by name and use professional language. Phishing emails often use generic greetings like "Dear Customer" and contain spelling or grammatical errors, which can be a red flag.

Be wary of unexpected attachments or links. Phishing emails often include malicious attachments or links that direct you to fraudulent websites designed to steal your information. Hover over links to see the URL before clicking, and avoid downloading attachments unless you are certain they are safe.

If you suspect an email might be a phishing attempt, do not respond, click on any links, or download any attachments. Instead, report the email to your email provider or the organization being impersonated. Many companies have dedicated channels for reporting phishing attempts and can take action to protect other customers.

Social Media Awareness

Social media platforms have become integral to our daily lives, but they also present risks. Being aware of these risks and taking steps to protect yourself can help you enjoy the benefits of social media without compromising your security.

One of the primary risks on social media is oversharing personal information. Cybercriminals can use the information you share publicly to build a profile of you and launch targeted attacks, such as phishing or identity theft. Avoid sharing sensitive information such as your home address, phone number, or financial details on social media. Be cautious about the personal details you include in your posts, comments, and profile information.

Adjusting your privacy settings is crucial for controlling who can see your information and interact with you on social media. Most platforms allow you to customize your privacy settings to limit who can view your posts, send you messages, and access your profile. Regularly review and update these settings to ensure that you are sharing information only with trusted contacts.

Be cautious of friend requests and messages from strangers. Cybercriminals often create fake profiles to connect with potential victims and gather information or spread malware. If you receive a friend request from someone you don't know or a message that seems suspicious, do not accept the request or engage with the message. Verify the person's identity through mutual friends or other means before adding them to your network.

Social media platforms are also used to spread scams and malware. Be wary of clicking on links or downloading files from social media, especially if they are from unknown or unverified sources. Scammers often use sensational headlines, fake news, or enticing offers to lure users into clicking on malicious links.

Be mindful of the applications and games you use on social media. Some third-party apps request access to your profile information and other personal data. Before granting permissions, review the app's privacy policy and ensure it is from a reputable developer. Limit the information you share with these apps and revoke access if you no longer use them.

Protecting Personal Information

Protecting your personal information online is essential for preventing identity theft, financial fraud, and other cybercrimes. Here are some strategies to help safeguard your personal information.

Use strong, unique passwords for each of your online accounts. Avoid reusing passwords across multiple sites, as this increases the risk of all your accounts being compromised if one password is breached. Password managers can help you generate and store complex passwords securely.

Enable multi-factor authentication (MFA) on your accounts whenever possible. MFA adds an extra layer of security by requiring you to provide two or more verification factors to access your account, such as a password and a code sent to your mobile device. This makes it much harder for cybercriminals to gain unauthorized access, even if they have your password.

Be cautious about sharing personal information online. Avoid posting sensitive details such as your social security number, financial information, or home address on public forums, social media, or unsecured websites. When required to provide personal information, ensure that the website is secure (look for HTTPS in the URL) and that you trust the entity requesting the information.

Regularly monitor your financial accounts and credit reports for unusual activity. Reviewing your bank statements, credit card bills, and credit reports can help you detect signs of identity theft or fraud early. If you notice any unauthorized transactions or accounts, report them to your financial institution and credit bureaus immediately.

Shred sensitive documents before disposing of them. Physical documents such as bank statements, tax returns, and medical records can contain personal information that identity thieves can use. Shredding these documents before discarding them can help protect your information.

Spotting Fake Profiles

Fake profiles on social media and other online platforms are often used by cybercriminals to deceive users, gather information, and spread malware. Being able to spot fake profiles can help you avoid falling victim to these schemes.

Fake profiles often use generic or stolen photos. Perform a reverse image search on the profile picture to see if it appears on multiple websites or is associated with different names. This can indicate that the photo has been taken from elsewhere and is being used to create a fake profile.

Check the profile's activity and connections. Fake profiles often have limited activity, few friends or followers, and generic posts. Look for signs of real-life interactions, such as comments from other users or tagged photos, which can indicate that the profile belongs to a genuine person.

Be cautious of profiles that send unsolicited friend requests or messages, especially if they immediately ask for personal information, financial assistance, or try to direct you to another website. Scammers often use fake profiles to initiate contact and build trust with potential victims.

Review the profile's content for inconsistencies. Fake profiles may have incomplete or contradictory information in their bio, posts, and comments. Look for details that do not add up or seem too good to be true, such as exaggerated claims about wealth or success.

If you suspect a profile is fake, report it to the platform's support team. Most social media sites have mechanisms for reporting suspicious profiles, which helps protect other users from potential scams.

Secure Transactions

Conducting secure transactions online is crucial for protecting your financial information and preventing fraud. Here are some best practices for ensuring secure transactions.

Use reputable websites and services for online purchases and financial transactions. Stick to well-known retailers and financial institutions with established security protocols. Before entering your payment information, verify that the website is secure by checking for HTTPS in the URL and looking for a padlock icon in the address bar.

Avoid using public Wi-Fi networks for financial transactions. Public Wi-Fi is often unsecured and can be exploited by cybercriminals to intercept your data. If you need to make a transaction while on the go, use your mobile data or a VPN to encrypt your connection and protect your information.

Monitor your accounts for unusual activity. Regularly reviewing your bank statements, credit card bills, and transaction history can help you detect unauthorized transactions early. If you notice any suspicious activity, report it to your financial institution immediately.

Use credit cards instead of debit cards for online purchases. Credit cards offer better fraud protection and are not directly linked to your bank account, which can limit the potential impact of unauthorized transactions. Many credit card companies also provide additional security features, such as virtual card numbers, to enhance online transaction security.

Be cautious of phishing attempts. Scammers often send emails or messages that appear to be from legitimate companies, asking you to update your payment information or confirm a transaction. Verify the authenticity of such requests by contacting the company directly using known contact information.

Ensuring Safe Online Purchases

Safe online purchases require careful attention to the security of the websites you use and the transactions you conduct. Here are some strategies to ensure your online purchases are secure.

Research the seller before making a purchase. Look for reviews and ratings from other customers to gauge the seller's reputation. If the seller is new or has few reviews, be cautious and consider purchasing from a more established retailer.

Verify the security of the website. Ensure that the website uses HTTPS encryption, which helps protect your data during transmission. Look for a padlock icon in the address bar and check the website's privacy policy and contact information to confirm its legitimacy.

Be cautious of deals that seem too good to be true. Scammers often lure victims with unbelievably low prices or limited-time offers. If an offer seems suspicious, research the product and seller to determine if it is genuine.

Use secure payment methods. Credit cards, PayPal, and other reputable payment services offer additional protection against fraud. Avoid using wire transfers, money orders, or other untraceable payment methods that make it difficult to recover your funds if something goes wrong.

Keep records of your transactions. Save copies of order confirmations, receipts, and correspondence with the seller. These records can be useful if you need to dispute a charge or report a problem with your purchase.

Avoiding Fake Websites

Fake websites are designed to look like legitimate sites to trick users into providing personal information, making purchases, or downloading malware. Here are some tips for avoiding fake websites.

Check the URL carefully. Fake websites often use URLs that are similar to those of legitimate sites but may include slight variations, such as misspellings or additional characters. Verify the URL and ensure it matches the official website of the company or organization.

Look for signs of a secure connection. Ensure that the website uses HTTPS encryption and that a padlock icon is present in the address bar. This indicates that the website uses secure protocols to protect your data.

Be cautious of pop-ups and ads. Fake websites often use aggressive pop-ups and ads to direct you to malicious sites or prompt you to download harmful software. Use a reputable ad blocker to reduce the risk of encountering these threats.

Verify the website's legitimacy through independent sources. Search for reviews, ratings, and information about the website from trusted sources. Be cautious of websites with little to no online presence or those that have been recently created.

Avoid clicking on links in unsolicited emails or messages. Scammers often use phishing emails to direct victims to fake websites. Instead, navigate to the website by typing the URL directly into your browser or using a bookmarked link.

Building Awareness and Resilience

Building awareness and resilience against online threats involves staying informed about the latest cyber threats and adopting best practices to protect yourself. Here are some strategies to build awareness and resilience:

Stay updated on cybersecurity news. Follow reputable sources for information on emerging threats, security breaches, and best practices for online safety. Being aware of the latest trends can help you recognize and respond to new threats.

Participate in cybersecurity training. Many organizations offer training programs and resources to help individuals and businesses enhance their cybersecurity knowledge. Participating in these programs can provide valuable insights and practical skills for protecting yourself online.

Share your knowledge with others. Educate friends, family members, and colleagues about online threats and safe practices. Raising awareness within your community can help others recognize and avoid scams.

Regularly review and update your security practices. Cyber threats constantly evolve, so it's important to periodically review and update your security measures. This includes changing passwords, updating software, and reassessing your online habits.

Create a security plan for your devices and accounts. Develop a comprehensive security plan that includes measures such as using strong passwords, enabling multi-factor authentication, and regularly backing up your data. Having a plan in place can help you respond effectively to potential threats.

Institutional and Community Efforts

While individual actions are crucial, institutional and community efforts play a significant role in enhancing online security. Organizations, businesses, and government agencies can implement measures to protect individuals and contribute to broader cybersecurity efforts.

Businesses can enhance their security practices and educate their customers about common online threats. Providing clear communication about company policies, such as never requesting personal information or payments through unusual methods, can help customers recognize fraudulent attempts. Offering resources and tools for customers to secure their accounts, such as transaction alerts and fraud detection services, can enhance protection.

Financial institutions are on the front lines of cybersecurity. Banks and credit card companies can monitor for unusual account activity and alert customers to potential fraud. Offering resources and tools for customers to secure their accounts, such as transaction alerts and fraud detection services, can enhance protection. Financial institutions can also collaborate with law enforcement to identify and shut down fraudulent operations.

Government agencies have a crucial role in regulating and enforcing cybersecurity laws. Establishing and enforcing consumer protection laws, investigating cybercrimes, and prosecuting cybercriminals are essential functions. Government agencies can also lead public awareness campaigns, providing information on how to recognize and report online threats. Collaboration with international agencies is important in addressing cross-border cybercrimes and enhancing global efforts to combat fraud.

Public awareness and education campaigns can reach a wide audience, providing valuable information on how to protect oneself online. Government agencies, consumer protection organizations, and community groups can collaborate to raise awareness through media, social networks, and community events. These campaigns can highlight current cyber threats, provide tips for recognizing red flags, and encourage individuals to report suspicious activities.

International collaboration is increasingly important in combating cyber threats that cross national borders. Cybercriminals often operate in multiple countries, making it challenging for individual nations to address the issue effectively. International cooperation, including information sharing, joint investigations, and coordinated enforcement actions, can enhance global efforts to combat cybercrimes.

Future Trends and Challenges

As technology and society continue to evolve, so do the tactics and methods of cybercriminals. Anticipating future trends in online threats can help individuals and institutions stay ahead of emerging risks and develop effective prevention strategies.

Artificial Intelligence (AI) and machine learning are likely to be leveraged by cybercriminals to create more sophisticated and convincing attacks. AI can analyze vast amounts of data to personalize phishing emails, making them more relevant and believable to each target. Deepfake technology, which creates realistic but fake audio and video, can be used to impersonate trusted individuals, adding another layer of deception.

Cybersecurity advancements will continue to play a crucial role in protecting against online threats. Developing and deploying advanced security technologies, such as biometric authentication and blockchain, can enhance protection against cybercrimes. However, as cybersecurity measures become more sophisticated, cybercriminals will also adapt, necessitating ongoing vigilance and innovation.

Global collaboration in fighting cybercrimes will become increasingly important. Cybercriminals often operate across borders, making it challenging for individual countries to address the issue effectively. International cooperation, including information sharing, joint investigations, and coordinated enforcement actions, will be essential in combating global cyber threats.

Public awareness and education will remain foundational in cybersecurity. As new threats emerge, continuous efforts to educate the public about these risks and how to avoid them will be necessary. Leveraging digital platforms and social media to reach a wide audience can enhance the effectiveness of awareness campaigns.

Protecting yourself online requires a comprehensive approach that includes safe internet practices, secure browsing habits, recognizing phishing emails, social media awareness, protecting personal information, spotting fake profiles, ensuring secure transactions, making safe online purchases, and avoiding fake websites. By adopting these practices and staying informed about the latest cyber threats, you can significantly reduce your risk of falling victim to online scams and cybercrimes.

Individual actions, such as using strong passwords, enabling multi-factor authentication, and being cautious with personal information, are crucial for maintaining online security. Institutional and community efforts, including public awareness campaigns, consumer protection laws, and international collaboration, play a significant role in creating a safer online environment.

Anticipating future trends and challenges in cyber threats can help individuals and institutions stay ahead of emerging risks and develop effective prevention strategies. By fostering a culture of awareness, vigilance, and resilience, we can protect ourselves and our communities from the harmful consequences of cybercrimes.

CHAPTER 5 DEALING WITH SCAMMERS

Encountering a scammer can be a distressing experience, but knowing how to respond effectively is crucial for minimizing potential harm. This chapter provides a comprehensive guide on what to do if you are targeted by a scam, how to report scams, and the legal recourse available to victims. By understanding these processes, you can better protect yourself and help prevent others from falling victim to similar schemes.

What to Do If Targeted

If you suspect that you are being targeted by a scammer, taking immediate and decisive action can prevent further damage. The first step is to remain calm and avoid acting impulsively. Scammers often create a sense of urgency to prompt quick decisions, so it is important to take a moment to assess the situation rationally.

Identify and document the scam: Take note of any details related to the scam, including the communication you received, the contact information of the scammer, and any instructions given. This documentation can be useful when reporting the scam to authorities and seeking legal recourse. Keep records of emails, text messages, phone calls, and any other interactions with the scammer.

Cease communication: Once you recognize that you are dealing with a scammer, stop all communication immediately. Engaging further can provide the scammer with more opportunities to manipulate and deceive you. Block the scammer's phone number, email address, and social media profiles to prevent further contact.

Secure your accounts and information: If you have provided any personal information to the scammer, take steps to secure your accounts. Change your passwords for email, banking, and other online accounts. Consider enabling multi-factor authentication to add an extra layer of security. If you suspect that your financial information has been compromised, contact your bank or credit card company to report the incident and take appropriate measures to protect your accounts.

Run antivirus and malware scans: If you clicked on any links or downloaded attachments from the scammer, run a thorough antivirus and malware scan on your devices. Cybercriminals often use these tactics to install malicious software that can steal your information or compromise your system.

Inform and seek advice from trusted sources: Discuss the situation with friends, family members, or colleagues. They can provide support, offer advice, and help you make informed decisions. Trusted individuals can also help you verify whether an interaction is legitimate or potentially fraudulent.

Report the scam: Reporting the scam to the relevant authorities is a crucial step in dealing with scammers. Many organizations have dedicated channels for reporting scams, and your report can help prevent others from falling victim.

Reporting Scams

Reporting scams is essential for combating fraud and protecting others from similar experiences. Various organizations and agencies accept scam reports and can take action to investigate and address fraudulent activities. Here are some key steps to take when reporting a scam:

Contact your local law enforcement: Filing a report with your local police department is an important step, especially if you have suffered financial loss or if the scam involves identity theft. Provide them with all the documentation and details you have collected about the scam. While local law enforcement may not always be able to resolve internet-based scams, they can offer advice and take necessary action within their jurisdiction.

Report to the Federal Trade Commission (FTC): The FTC collects information about scams and uses it to track and combat fraudulent activities. You can file a complaint with the FTC online through their website. The FTC also provides resources and advice for scam victims, helping you understand your rights and the steps you can take to protect yourself.

Notify the Internet Crime Complaint Center (IC3): Operated by the FBI, the IC3 is a central hub for reporting internet-based crimes, including scams. Filing a complaint with the IC3 helps federal law enforcement agencies investigate and address online fraud. The IC3 website provides detailed instructions on how to file a complaint and what information to include.

Contact your bank or credit card company: If you provided financial information to the scammer, notify your bank or credit card company immediately. They can take steps to protect your accounts, such as freezing your account, issuing a new credit card, or monitoring for suspicious activity. Financial institutions often have fraud departments dedicated to handling such incidents.

Report to the Better Business Bureau (BBB): The BBB collects information about business-related scams and helps consumers resolve disputes with businesses. Filing a complaint with the BBB can help warn others about fraudulent businesses and contribute to the organization's efforts to combat scams.

Notify relevant online platforms: If the scam occurred through a specific website, social media platform, or email service, report the incident to the platform's support team. Most platforms have mechanisms for reporting scams, fake profiles, and fraudulent activities. By reporting the scam, you can help the platform take action to remove the scammer and protect other users.

Contact identity theft protection services: If you believe your personal information has been compromised, consider enrolling in an identity theft protection service. These services can help monitor your credit reports, alert you to suspicious activity, and assist you in recovering from identity theft.

Legal Recourse

Victims of scams may have legal recourse to recover their losses and seek justice. Understanding your legal options can help you take appropriate action and potentially hold scammers accountable for their actions. Here are some key considerations for pursuing legal recourse:

Consult with a lawyer: Seeking legal advice from a lawyer experienced in fraud and consumer protection can provide you with valuable insights into your options. A lawyer can help you understand your rights, assess the strength of your case, and guide you through the legal process. They can also represent you in court if necessary.

File a civil lawsuit: In some cases, you may be able to file a civil lawsuit against the scammer to recover your losses. A civil lawsuit allows you to seek monetary damages for the harm you have suffered. To succeed in a civil lawsuit, you will need to provide evidence of the scam, such as documentation of communications, financial transactions, and other relevant details. While winning a civil lawsuit does not guarantee that you will be able to collect the awarded damages, it can be a way to hold the scammer accountable.

Pursue criminal charges: If the scam involves criminal activities, such as fraud, identity theft, or cybercrime, law enforcement agencies may pursue criminal charges against the scammer. Criminal charges can result in penalties such as fines, restitution, and imprisonment. While the decision to pursue criminal charges rests with law enforcement and prosecutors, providing them with detailed information about the scam can aid in their investigation.

Join a class action lawsuit: If the scam is part of a larger scheme that has affected multiple victims, you may have the option to join a class action lawsuit. A class action lawsuit allows a group of victims to collectively seek damages from the scammer. This can be an effective way to pool resources and increase the chances of holding the scammer accountable. Class action lawsuits are typically led by lawyers who specialize in representing large groups of plaintiffs.

Seek restitution through consumer protection agencies: Some consumer protection agencies and government organizations offer restitution programs for scam victims. These programs may provide financial compensation or assistance in recovering losses. Contacting agencies such as the FTC, state consumer protection offices, and other relevant organizations can help you determine if you are eligible for restitution.

Consider alternative dispute resolution (ADR): Alternative dispute resolution methods, such as mediation and arbitration, can provide a way to resolve disputes with scammers without going to court. ADR can be faster and less costly than traditional litigation. In mediation, a neutral third party helps both sides reach a mutually acceptable agreement. In arbitration, a neutral arbitrator hears the case and makes a binding decision. While ADR may not be suitable for all situations, it can be an option for resolving certain types of scams.

Stay informed about legal developments: Laws and regulations related to scams and consumer protection are continually evolving. Staying informed about legal developments can help you understand your rights and the protections available to you. Government websites, legal resources, and consumer advocacy organizations are valuable sources of information.

Case Studies: Dealing with Scammers

Examining real-life examples of individuals who have dealt with scammers can provide valuable insights into the steps they took and the outcomes they achieved. These case studies highlight the importance of taking prompt action, reporting scams, and seeking legal recourse.

Case Study 1: Jane's Experience with a Phishing Scam

Jane, a small business owner, received an email that appeared to be from her bank, claiming that her account had been compromised and she needed to update her login credentials. The email included a link to a website that looked identical to her bank's login page. Unaware that it was a phishing scam, Jane entered her username and password.

Shortly after, Jane noticed unauthorized transactions in her bank account. Realizing she had been scammed, she immediately contacted her bank to report the fraud and secure her account. The bank froze her account, issued a new card, and reimbursed the unauthorized charges.

Jane then reported the phishing email to the FTC and the IC3. She also notified her local law enforcement and provided them with all the details of the scam. With the support of her bank and the authorities, Jane was able to recover her funds and protect her business from further harm.

Case Study 2: Mark's Battle with a Tech Support Scam

Mark received a pop-up message on his computer claiming that his system was infected with a virus and that he needed to call Microsoft support immediately. The message included a phone number and urged him to act quickly. Concerned about his computer's security, Mark called the number and spoke with "John," who claimed to be a Microsoft technician.

John instructed Mark to download a remote access tool, which allowed him to control Mark's computer. He then showed Mark several fake error messages and claimed that his computer was severely compromised. John offered to fix the issues for a fee, and Mark provided his credit card information to make the payment.

After realizing that his computer was still experiencing issues and suspecting that he had been scammed, Mark contacted

Microsoft directly and learned that the pop-up message and support call were fraudulent. He immediately canceled his credit card and reported the scam to the FTC, IC3, and his local law enforcement. Mark also ran antivirus and malware scans on his computer to remove any malicious software installed by the scammer.

With the help of the authorities and his credit card company, Mark was able to minimize the financial damage and secure his computer. He also educated himself about common tech support scams to avoid similar incidents in the future.

Case Study 3: Susan's Recovery from a Romance Scam

Susan, a widow in her 60s, met "David" on an online dating site. David claimed to be a successful businessman working overseas. Over several months, they developed a deep emotional connection, exchanging messages and phone calls regularly. David eventually told Susan that he was facing a financial crisis and needed money to resolve the situation.

Wanting to help, Susan wired several thousand dollars to David. When David's requests for money continued and his stories became more elaborate, Susan grew suspicious and confided in her daughter. Her daughter conducted a reverse image search of David's profile picture and found it associated with multiple scam reports.

Realizing she had been scammed, Susan immediately stopped all communication with David and reported the incident to the dating site. She also filed reports with the FTC, IC3, and her local law enforcement. While the chances of recovering her money were slim, Susan's actions helped protect others from falling victim to the same scammer.

Susan also sought emotional support from friends, family, and a therapist to cope with the feelings of betrayal and loss. By sharing her experience, she raised awareness about romance scams and encouraged others to be cautious when forming online relationships.

Building Awareness and Resilience

Building awareness and resilience against scams involves staying informed about the latest fraud tactics, adopting best practices for protecting yourself, and seeking support when needed. Here are some strategies to build awareness and resilience:

Stay updated on scam trends: Follow reputable sources for information on emerging scams and fraud tactics. Government websites, consumer protection agencies, and news outlets provide valuable updates and resources.

Participate in fraud prevention programs: Many organizations offer training and resources to help individuals and businesses enhance their fraud prevention knowledge. Participating in these programs can provide practical skills for recognizing and responding to scams.

Share your knowledge with others: Educate friends, family members, and colleagues about common scams and how to avoid them. Raising awareness within your community can help others recognize and avoid fraudulent activities.

Develop critical thinking skills: Practice critical thinking and skepticism when evaluating offers and requests. Question the legitimacy of too-good-to-be-true offers, verify the authenticity of urgent requests, and be cautious of unusual payment methods.

Create a support network: Build a network of trusted

individuals with whom you can discuss suspicious situations. Consulting others can provide different perspectives and help identify potential red flags.

Implement robust security measures: Use strong passwords, enable multi-factor authentication, and regularly monitor your accounts for unusual activity. Taking proactive steps to secure your personal and financial information can reduce your risk of falling victim to scams.

Institutional and Community Efforts

While individual actions are crucial, institutional and community efforts play a significant role in combating scams and protecting victims. Organizations, businesses, and government agencies can implement measures to enhance fraud prevention and support scam victims.

Businesses can improve their security practices and educate customers about common scams. Providing clear communication about company policies, such as never requesting personal information or payments through unusual methods, can help customers recognize fraudulent attempts. Offering resources and tools for customers to secure their accounts, such as transaction alerts and fraud detection services, can enhance protection.

Financial institutions are on the front lines of fraud prevention. Banks and credit card companies can monitor for unusual account activity and alert customers to potential scams. Offering resources and tools for customers to secure their accounts, such as transaction alerts and fraud detection services, can enhance protection. Financial institutions can also collaborate with law enforcement to identify and shut down fraudulent operations.

Government agencies play a crucial role in regulating and enforcing fraud prevention laws. Establishing and enforcing consumer protection laws, investigating scams, and prosecuting scammers are essential functions. Government agencies can also lead public awareness campaigns, providing information on how to recognize and report scams. Collaboration with international agencies is important in addressing cross-border scams and enhancing global efforts to combat fraud.

Public awareness and education campaigns can reach a wide audience, providing valuable information on how to protect oneself from scams. Government agencies, consumer protection organizations, and community groups can collaborate to raise awareness through media, social networks, and community events. These campaigns can highlight current scam trends, provide tips for recognizing red flags, and encourage individuals to report suspicious activities.

International collaboration is increasingly important in combating scams that cross national borders. Scammers often operate in multiple countries, making it challenging for individual nations to address the issue effectively. International cooperation, including information sharing, joint investigations, and coordinated enforcement actions, can enhance global efforts to combat fraud.

Future Trends and Challenges

As technology and society continue to evolve, so do the tactics and methods of scammers. Anticipating future trends in fraud can help individuals and institutions stay ahead of emerging threats and develop effective prevention strategies.

Artificial Intelligence (AI) and machine learning are likely to be leveraged by scammers to create more sophisticated and convincing fraud schemes. AI can analyze vast amounts of data to personalize phishing emails, making them more relevant and believable to each target. Deepfake technology, which creates realistic but fake audio and video, can be used to impersonate trusted individuals, adding another layer of deception.

Cybersecurity advancements will continue to play a crucial role in protecting against fraud. Developing and deploying advanced security technologies, such as biometric authentication and blockchain, can enhance protection against scams. However, as cybersecurity measures become more sophisticated, scammers will also adapt, necessitating ongoing vigilance and innovation.

Global collaboration in fighting fraud will become increasingly important. Scammers often operate across borders, making it challenging for individual countries to address the issue effectively. International cooperation, including information sharing, joint investigations, and coordinated enforcement actions, will be essential in combating global fraud.

Public awareness and education will remain foundational in fraud prevention. As new scams emerge, continuous efforts to educate the public about these risks and how to avoid them will be necessary. Leveraging digital platforms and social media to reach a wide audience can enhance the effectiveness of awareness campaigns.

Dealing with scammers involves a multi-faceted approach that includes knowing what to do if targeted, reporting scams, and understanding legal recourse. By staying informed, taking prompt action, and seeking support, individuals can protect themselves and help prevent others from falling victim to fraud.

Individual actions, such as documenting the scam, ceasing communication, securing accounts, and reporting the incident, are crucial for minimizing harm. Institutional and community efforts, including public awareness campaigns, consumer protection laws, and international collaboration, play a significant role in combating scams and supporting victims.

Anticipating future trends and challenges in fraud can help individuals and institutions stay ahead of emerging threats and develop effective prevention strategies. By fostering a culture of awareness, vigilance, and resilience, we can protect ourselves and our communities from the harmful consequences of scams.

CHAPTER 6
PREVENTATIVE
MEASURES

Preventative measures are essential for safeguarding against scams and cyber threats. By educating yourself and others, implementing financial safeguards, using secure payment methods, monitoring accounts, and leveraging technology tools, you can build a robust defense against potential fraud. This chapter delves into various strategies and tools that can help you protect your personal and financial information from malicious actors.

Educating Yourself and Others

Education is the cornerstone of prevention. Understanding the tactics used by scammers and staying informed about the latest threats can significantly reduce your risk of falling victim to fraud. Additionally, sharing this knowledge with others can create a more informed and vigilant community.

Stay Informed: Regularly update yourself on the latest scams and cybersecurity threats. Follow reputable sources such as government agencies, consumer protection organizations, and cybersecurity experts. Websites like the Federal Trade Commission (FTC), the Better Business Bureau (BBB), and the Internet Crime Complaint Center (IC3) provide valuable information on emerging scams and how to avoid them.

Subscribing to newsletters, alerts, and blogs from these sources can keep you informed about current threats.

Participate in Training Programs: Many organizations offer cybersecurity training and awareness programs. These programs can provide practical skills for recognizing and responding to scams. For example, the FTC offers resources and tools for consumers to learn about different types of scams and how to protect themselves. Similarly, cybersecurity firms often provide webinars, workshops, and online courses on topics such as phishing, identity theft, and safe online practices.

Community Engagement: Share your knowledge with friends, family members, and colleagues. Encourage open discussions about online safety and fraud prevention. Hosting or participating in community events, such as seminars or workshops, can help spread awareness. Schools, workplaces, and community centers can also play a crucial role in educating individuals about cybersecurity.

Use Real-Life Examples: Illustrating scams with real-life examples can make the information more relatable and impactful. Case studies of victims who have encountered scams can highlight the tactics used by scammers and the steps taken to mitigate the damage. These examples can serve as powerful reminders of the importance of vigilance and caution.

Promote Critical Thinking: Encourage critical thinking and skepticism when evaluating offers, requests, or communications. Teach others to question the legitimacy of too-good-to-be-true offers, verify the authenticity of urgent requests, and be cautious of unusual payment methods. Developing a habit of analyzing and verifying information can help individuals make informed decisions and avoid falling prey to scams.

Financial Safeguards

Implementing financial safeguards is crucial for protecting your assets from fraud. By adopting best practices for managing your finances, you can reduce the risk of unauthorized transactions and financial loss.

Use Strong Passwords: Protect your financial accounts with strong, unique passwords. A strong password should include a combination of upper and lowercase letters, numbers, and special characters. Avoid using easily guessable information such as your name, birthdate, or common words. Consider using a password manager to generate and store complex passwords securely.

Enable Multi-Factor Authentication (MFA): MFA adds an extra layer of security to your accounts by requiring two or more verification factors to gain access. This could include something you know (a password), something you have (a mobile device), or something you are (biometric authentication). Enabling MFA on your banking, credit card, and investment accounts can significantly enhance security.

Regularly Monitor Your Accounts: Routinely check your bank statements, credit card bills, and transaction history for any unusual activity. Promptly report any unauthorized transactions to your financial institution. Many banks and credit card companies offer account alerts that notify you of suspicious activity, enabling you to take immediate action.

Use Credit Cards for Online Purchases: Credit cards offer better fraud protection than debit cards. If a fraudulent transaction occurs, credit card companies are more likely to reimburse the charges. Additionally, credit cards are not directly linked to your bank account, which can limit the potential impact of unauthorized transactions.

Set Up Account Alerts: Many financial institutions offer alerts that notify you of specific activities, such as large transactions, changes to account information, or low balances. Setting up these alerts can help you quickly identify and respond to potential fraud.

Consider a Credit Freeze: A credit freeze restricts access to your credit report, making it difficult for identity thieves to open new accounts in your name. You can temporarily lift the freeze if you need to apply for credit. Contact the major credit bureaus (Equifax, Experian, and TransUnion) to place a freeze on your credit.

Secure Payment Methods

Using secure payment methods can help protect your financial information during transactions. By choosing reputable payment services and understanding the risks associated with different methods, you can reduce the likelihood of fraud.

Credit Cards: As mentioned earlier, credit cards offer strong consumer protections and are generally safer for online purchases than debit cards. Most credit card companies provide fraud detection services and zero-liability policies for unauthorized transactions.

Payment Services: Reputable payment services such as PayPal, Apple Pay, and Google Pay offer secure payment options for online transactions. These services often use encryption and tokenization to protect your payment information. Additionally, they may offer dispute resolution services if you encounter issues with a transaction.

Virtual Credit Cards: Some banks and credit card companies offer virtual credit cards, which generate temporary card numbers for online purchases. These numbers are linked to your actual credit card but provide an added layer of security by masking your real card number.

Avoid Untraceable Payment Methods: Be cautious of sellers or services that request payment via wire transfers, money orders, or cryptocurrency. These payment methods are difficult to trace and often used by scammers. Stick to payment methods that offer protection and recourse in case of fraud.

Verify Payment Requests: Always verify the legitimacy of payment requests, especially if they come from unsolicited emails or messages. Contact the company or individual directly using known contact information to confirm the request before making a payment.

Monitoring Accounts

Regularly monitoring your financial and online accounts is essential for detecting and responding to unauthorized activity. By staying vigilant, you can quickly identify potential fraud and take appropriate action.

Review Statements and Transactions: Routinely review your bank statements, credit card bills, and transaction history for any unusual or unauthorized activity. Promptly report any discrepancies to your financial institution. Keeping a close eye on your accounts can help you detect fraud early and minimize its impact.

Set Up Account Alerts: Many financial institutions offer alerts that notify you of specific activities, such as large transactions, changes to account information, or low balances. Setting up these alerts can help you quickly identify and respond to potential fraud.

Check Your Credit Report: Regularly review your credit report for any signs of identity theft, such as new accounts you did not open or inquiries you did not authorize. You are entitled to a free credit report from each of the major credit bureaus (Equifax, Experian, and TransUnion) once a year. Stagger your requests to review your credit report every four months.

Monitor Your Online Accounts: In addition to financial accounts, monitor your online accounts for any unusual activity. This includes email, social media, and other online services. If you notice any suspicious activity, change your password immediately and enable multi-factor authentication.

Use Identity Theft Protection Services: Consider enrolling in an identity theft protection service. These services can monitor your credit reports, alert you to suspicious activity, and assist you in recovering from identity theft. Some services also offer insurance to cover expenses related to identity theft.

Technology Tools

Leveraging technology tools can enhance your security and protect your personal information from cyber threats. By using antivirus software, VPNs, and other security tools, you can create a more secure online environment.

Anti-Virus Software: Installing reputable antivirus software on your devices can help protect against malware, viruses, and other cyber threats. Antivirus software scans your system for malicious code and provides real-time protection against new threats. Keep your antivirus software up to date to ensure it can detect and respond to the latest threats.

VPNs (Virtual Private Networks): A VPN encrypts your internet connection and masks your IP address, providing privacy and security when browsing the web. Using a VPN is especially important when accessing the internet on public Wi-Fi networks, which are often unsecured and vulnerable to cyberattacks. By encrypting your connection, a VPN helps protect your data from interception and eavesdropping.

Firewalls: A firewall acts as a barrier between your device and the internet, blocking unauthorized access and protecting your system from cyber threats. Many operating systems come with built-in firewalls, but you can also install third-party firewall software for additional protection. Ensure that your firewall is enabled and properly configured to safeguard your network.

Password Managers: Password managers help you generate and store strong, unique passwords for each of your online accounts. By using a password manager, you can avoid the risks associated with reusing passwords or using weak passwords. Many password managers also offer features such as secure password sharing, encrypted storage for sensitive information, and automatic form filling.

Encryption Tools: Encryption tools can help protect your sensitive data by converting it into unreadable code that can only be accessed with a decryption key. Using encryption tools for your files, emails, and communications can provide an additional layer of security. Many services, such as email providers and cloud storage platforms, offer built-in encryption options.

Secure Browsers and Extensions: Using secure web browsers and privacy-focused extensions can enhance your online security. Browsers such as Mozilla Firefox and Google Chrome offer robust security features, including built-in phishing and malware protection. Privacy-focused extensions, such as ad blockers, anti-tracking tools, and script blockers, can further protect your browsing experience.

Anti-Virus Software

Anti-virus software is a critical component of your cybersecurity toolkit. It helps protect your devices from malware, viruses, ransomware, and other malicious software that can compromise your data and security.

Choosing Anti-Virus Software: Select reputable anti-virus software from trusted providers. Look for software that offers comprehensive protection, including real-time scanning, automatic updates, and advanced threat detection. Popular anti-virus software providers include Norton, McAfee, Bitdefender, Kaspersky, and Avast.

Regular Scanning: Schedule regular scans of your devices to detect and remove any malicious software. Most anti-virus software allows you to set up automatic scans at regular intervals. In addition to scheduled scans, perform manual scans if you suspect that your device may be infected.

Real-Time Protection: Ensure that your anti-virus software provides real-time protection, which continuously monitors your system for threats and blocks malicious activities as they occur. Real-time protection can help prevent malware from being installed and stop ongoing attacks.

Update Definitions: Keep your anti-virus software up to date by regularly updating its virus definitions. Cybercriminals constantly develop new malware, and updates ensure that your software can recognize and protect against the latest threats.

Multi-Device Protection: Consider anti-virus software that offers multi-device protection, especially if you use multiple devices such as computers, smartphones, and tablets. Protecting all your devices with the same anti-virus software can provide consistent security and simplify management.

VPNs (Virtual Private Networks)

A VPN enhances your online privacy and security by encrypting your internet connection and masking your IP address. Using a VPN can protect your data from interception, especially when using public Wi-Fi networks.

Choosing a VPN: Select a reputable VPN provider that offers strong encryption, a no-logs policy, and a wide range of server locations. Look for VPNs that provide user-friendly applications, high-speed connections, and reliable customer support. Popular

VPN providers include ExpressVPN, NordVPN, CyberGhost, and Private Internet Access.

Installing and Configuring a VPN: Install the VPN application on your devices and follow the provider's instructions for configuration. Most VPN applications offer easy setup processes and intuitive interfaces. Configure the VPN to automatically connect when you start your device or when you connect to an unsecured network.

Using a VPN: Activate the VPN whenever you access the internet, especially on public Wi-Fi networks. The VPN will encrypt your internet traffic, making it difficult for cybercriminals to intercept and access your data. Using a VPN can also help protect your privacy by masking your IP address and preventing websites from tracking your location.

Benefits Beyond Security: In addition to enhancing security, VPNs can provide other benefits, such as bypassing geo-restrictions and accessing content that may be blocked in your region. VPNs can also help protect against censorship and provide a more open internet experience.

Two-Factor Authentication

Two-factor authentication (2FA) adds an extra layer of security to your online accounts by requiring two forms of verification. This can include something you know (a password) and something you have (a code sent to your mobile device) or something you are (biometric authentication).

Enabling 2FA: Enable 2FA on your online accounts whenever possible. Most major online services, including email providers, social media platforms, and financial institutions, offer 2FA options. Follow the service's instructions to enable 2FA and choose your preferred verification method.

Verification Methods: Common 2FA methods include SMS codes, authentication apps, and biometric authentication. SMS codes are sent to your mobile device, while authentication apps (such as Google Authenticator or Authy) generate time-based codes. Biometric authentication can include fingerprint or facial recognition.

Backup Options: Set up backup options for 2FA in case you lose access to your primary verification method. This can include backup codes, alternative phone numbers, or additional authentication methods. Storing backup codes in a secure location can help you regain access to your account if needed.

Benefits of 2FA: 2FA provides an additional layer of security, making it more difficult for cybercriminals to access your accounts. Even if your password is compromised, the second verification factor can prevent unauthorized access. Enabling 2FA can significantly reduce the risk of account breaches and protect your personal information.

Building Awareness and Resilience

Building awareness and resilience against cyber threats involves adopting a proactive approach to security and staying informed about the latest trends and best practices.

Stay Updated on Cybersecurity News: Follow reputable sources for information on emerging threats, security breaches, and best practices for online safety. Government websites, cybersecurity firms, and consumer protection organizations provide valuable updates and resources.

Participate in Training Programs: Many organizations offer cybersecurity training and awareness programs. These programs can provide practical skills for recognizing and responding to cyber threats. Participating in webinars, workshops, and online courses can enhance your cybersecurity knowledge.

Share Your Knowledge: Educate friends, family members, and colleagues about common cyber threats and how to protect themselves. Raising awareness within your community can help others recognize and avoid scams and cyberattacks.

Develop Critical Thinking Skills: Practice critical thinking and skepticism when evaluating online offers, requests, and communications. Question the legitimacy of too-good-to-be-true offers, verify the authenticity of urgent requests, and be cautious of unusual payment methods.

Create a Support Network: Build a network of trusted individuals with whom you can discuss suspicious situations. Consulting others can provide different perspectives and help identify potential red flags.

Implement Robust Security Measures: Use strong passwords, enable multi-factor authentication, and regularly monitor your accounts for unusual activity. Taking proactive steps to secure your personal and financial information can reduce your risk of falling victim to cyber threats.

Institutional and Community Efforts

While individual actions are crucial, institutional and community efforts play a significant role in enhancing cybersecurity and protecting individuals from cyber threats. Organizations, businesses, and government agencies can implement measures to promote cybersecurity awareness and support victims of cybercrime.

Businesses: Improve security practices and educate customers about common cyber threats. Providing clear communication about company policies, such as never requesting personal information or payments through unusual methods, can help customers recognize fraudulent attempts. Offering resources and tools for customers to secure their accounts, such as transaction alerts and fraud detection services, can enhance protection.

Financial Institutions: Monitor for unusual account activity and alert customers to potential fraud. Offering resources and tools for customers to secure their accounts, such as transaction alerts and fraud detection services, can enhance protection. Financial institutions can also collaborate with law enforcement to identify and shut down fraudulent operations.

Government Agencies: Play a crucial role in regulating and enforcing cybersecurity laws. Establishing and enforcing consumer protection laws, investigating cybercrimes, and prosecuting cybercriminals are essential functions. Government agencies can also lead public awareness campaigns, providing information on how to recognize and report cyber threats. Collaboration with international agencies is important in addressing cross-border cybercrimes and enhancing global efforts to combat fraud.

Public Awareness and Education Campaigns: Reach a wide audience, providing valuable information on how to protect oneself from cyber threats. Government agencies, consumer protection organizations, and community groups can collaborate to raise awareness through media, social networks, and community events. These campaigns can highlight current cyber threats, provide tips for recognizing red flags, and encourage individuals to report suspicious activities.

International Collaboration: Increasingly important in combating cyber threats that cross national borders. Cybercriminals often operate in multiple countries, making it challenging for individual nations to address the issue effectively. International cooperation, including information sharing, joint investigations, and coordinated enforcement actions, can enhance global efforts to combat cybercrimes.

Future Trends and Challenges

As technology and society continue to evolve, so do the tactics and methods of cybercriminals. Anticipating future trends in cyber threats can help individuals and institutions stay ahead of emerging risks and develop effective prevention strategies.

Artificial Intelligence (AI) and Machine Learning: Likely to be leveraged by cybercriminals to create more sophisticated and convincing attacks. AI can analyze vast amounts of data to personalize phishing emails, making them more relevant and believable to each target. Deepfake technology, which creates realistic but fake audio and video, can be used to impersonate trusted individuals, adding another layer of deception.

Cybersecurity Advancements: Will continue to play a crucial role in protecting against cyber threats. Developing and deploying advanced security technologies, such as biometric authentication and blockchain, can enhance protection against cybercrimes. However, as cybersecurity measures become more sophisticated, cybercriminals will also adapt, necessitating ongoing vigilance and innovation.

Global Collaboration: Fighting cybercrimes will become increasingly important. Cybercriminals often operate across borders, making it challenging for individual countries to address the issue effectively. International cooperation, including information sharing, joint investigations, and coordinated enforcement actions, will be essential in combating global cyber threats.

Public Awareness and Education: Will remain foundational in cybersecurity. As new threats emerge, continuous efforts to educate the public about these risks and how to avoid them will be necessary. Leveraging digital platforms and social media to reach a wide audience can enhance the effectiveness of awareness campaigns.

Preventative measures are essential for safeguarding against scams and cyber threats. By educating yourself and others, implementing financial safeguards, using secure payment methods, monitoring accounts, and leveraging technology tools, you can build a robust defense against potential fraud.

Individual actions, such as staying informed, using strong passwords, enabling multi-factor authentication, and regularly monitoring accounts, are crucial for maintaining online security. Institutional and community efforts, including public awareness campaigns, consumer protection laws, and international collaboration, play a significant role in creating a safer online environment.

Anticipating future trends and challenges in cyber threats can help individuals and institutions stay ahead of emerging risks and develop effective prevention strategies. By fostering a culture of awareness, vigilance, and resilience, we can protect ourselves and our communities from the harmful consequences of cybercrimes.

CHAPTER 7 SCAMS TARGETING SPECIFIC GROUPS

Certain populations are more susceptible to specific types of scams due to their unique vulnerabilities and circumstances. This chapter focuses on the elderly and other vulnerable populations, businesses, and students, exploring common scams that target these groups, and offering detailed strategies to protect them from fraud.

Elderly and Vulnerable Populations

Elderly individuals are often prime targets for scammers due to factors such as social isolation, cognitive decline, and unfamiliarity with modern technology. Understanding the common scams that target the elderly and implementing protective measures can significantly reduce their risk of falling victim to fraud.

Common Scams Targeting the Elderly

One of the most prevalent scams targeting the elderly is the **grandparent scam**. In this scam, a fraudster poses as the victim's grandchild in distress, often claiming to be in a foreign country and needing money for bail, medical expenses, or travel. The scammer may instruct the victim not to inform other family members, creating a sense of urgency and secrecy. The emotional manipulation involved in this scam can make it highly effective, as elderly individuals may act quickly out of concern for their loved ones.

Another common scam is the **Medicare scam**, where scammers impersonate Medicare representatives to steal personal information or money. They might claim that the victim needs to update their Medicare information or purchase a new medical device. By providing personal information or making a payment, the victim unknowingly hands over sensitive data to the scammer.

Investment scams are also prevalent among the elderly. Scammers often present fraudulent investment opportunities promising high returns with little or no risk. These schemes can range from Ponzi schemes to fake real estate deals. The promise of financial security can be particularly enticing to elderly individuals looking to safeguard their retirement savings.

Telemarketing scams exploit the trust and politeness of elderly individuals. Scammers may call offering fake products or services, such as home repairs, insurance policies, or lottery winnings. The victim is asked to make a payment or provide personal information over the phone. These scams can be particularly difficult to detect, as they often rely on convincing and professional-sounding pitches.

Romance scams target elderly individuals who may be lonely and seeking companionship. Scammers create fake profiles on dating sites or social media platforms, build a relationship with the victim, and eventually request money for various emergencies. The emotional attachment formed in these scams can make the victim more willing to provide financial assistance.

How to Protect the Elderly and Vulnerable Populations

Protecting the elderly and other vulnerable populations from scams requires a multifaceted approach that includes education, vigilance, and support networks.

Education and Awareness: Educating elderly individuals about common scams and how they operate is crucial. Community centers, senior living facilities, and family members can organize informational sessions and provide resources on scam prevention. Materials should be clear and easy to understand, highlighting red flags and emphasizing the importance of skepticism.

Communication and Support Networks: Encouraging open communication between elderly individuals and their family members or caregivers can help identify potential scams early. Regular check-ins and discussions about financial decisions can provide opportunities to detect and prevent fraud. Creating a support network where elderly individuals feel comfortable discussing suspicious activities can significantly enhance their protection.

Setting Up Safeguards: Implementing financial safeguards, such as setting up account alerts, monitoring bank statements, and using direct deposit for Social Security or pension payments, can help detect unauthorized transactions. Family members or trusted individuals can assist with managing finances and ensuring that unusual activities are promptly addressed.

Encouraging Verification: Emphasize the importance of verifying any unsolicited requests for money or personal information. Encourage elderly individuals to contact family members, trusted friends, or official organizations directly to confirm the legitimacy of such requests before taking any action. Providing a list of verified contact numbers for banks, Medicare, and other relevant entities can be helpful.

Legal and Technological Measures: Consider using legal tools such as power of attorney to allow a trusted individual to manage financial affairs. Additionally, technological measures such as call blocking services, spam filters, and antivirus software can help reduce exposure to potential scams.

Business Scams

Businesses, particularly small and medium-sized enterprises (SMEs), are frequently targeted by scammers due to their often limited resources and lack of dedicated cybersecurity teams. Understanding the common scams targeting businesses and implementing protective measures can help safeguard company assets and reputation.

Common Business Scams

One prevalent scam is the **business email compromise (BEC)** scam. In this type of fraud, cybercriminals gain access to a company email account and use it to send fraudulent emails to employees, customers, or partners. These emails typically request payments, sensitive information, or changes to payment details. The scammer may impersonate a high-level executive, creating a sense of urgency and authority that prompts quick compliance.

Invoice scams involve scammers sending fake invoices to businesses, hoping that the payment will be made without thorough verification. These invoices often appear legitimate, complete with company logos and professional formatting. Small businesses with less rigorous accounting procedures are particularly vulnerable to this type of fraud.

Phishing attacks are another common threat to businesses. Cybercriminals send emails that appear to be from legitimate sources, such as vendors, customers, or government agencies, to trick employees into revealing login credentials or downloading malware. Phishing attacks can lead to data breaches, financial loss, and reputational damage.

Executive impersonation scams target businesses by impersonating a company executive, such as the CEO or CFO. The scammer typically sends an urgent email to an employee in the finance department, requesting an immediate wire transfer for a critical business transaction. The sense of urgency and authority often leads to the employee complying without verifying the request.

Tech support scams also affect businesses. Scammers pose as IT support and contact employees, claiming that there is a security issue with the company's network or devices. They then trick the employee into providing remote access to their computer, allowing the scammer to steal sensitive information or install malware.

Protecting Your Business from Fraud

Protecting your business from fraud requires a proactive approach that includes implementing robust security measures, fostering a culture of vigilance, and educating employees.

Employee Training and Awareness: Regularly educate employees about common scams and cybersecurity best practices. Training programs should cover how to recognize phishing emails, the importance of verifying requests, and the proper procedures for reporting suspicious activities. Encouraging a culture of vigilance and open communication can help employees feel comfortable reporting potential scams.

Implementing Security Protocols: Establish and enforce security protocols for handling financial transactions, accessing sensitive information, and communicating with external parties. This includes requiring multiple levels of approval for large transactions, using secure payment methods, and implementing multi-factor authentication for accessing company accounts.

Email Security Measures: Use email security solutions to detect and block phishing attempts and malicious attachments. Implement email authentication protocols such as SPF, DKIM, and DMARC to verify the legitimacy of incoming emails. Educating employees on how to identify and handle suspicious emails is also crucial.

Regular Audits and Monitoring: Conduct regular audits of financial transactions and account activities to identify any discrepancies or unauthorized actions. Monitoring software can help detect unusual behavior, such as large or frequent transfers to unfamiliar accounts.

Securing IT Infrastructure: Invest in cybersecurity solutions such as firewalls, antivirus software, and intrusion detection systems to protect your network and devices. Regularly update software and systems to patch vulnerabilities and reduce the risk of cyberattacks. Implementing strong access controls and using encryption for sensitive data can further enhance security.

Establishing Vendor Verification Processes: Implement verification processes for dealing with vendors and suppliers. This includes confirming payment details through trusted communication channels, verifying the legitimacy of invoices, and maintaining a list of approved vendors. Encouraging employees to verify any changes in payment instructions directly with the vendor can help prevent invoice scams.

Legal and Insurance Protections: Consider obtaining cybersecurity insurance to cover potential losses from fraud and cyberattacks. Legal measures such as drafting clear policies on handling financial transactions and protecting sensitive information can also provide a framework for responding to scams.

Student Scams

Students, particularly those in higher education, are often targeted by scammers due to their limited experience with financial management and the pressure to secure funding for their education. Understanding the common scams targeting students and implementing protective measures can help them navigate their financial responsibilities safely.

Common Student Scams

One of the most prevalent scams targeting students is the **student loan scam**. Scammers pose as representatives from loan consolidation or forgiveness programs, offering to help students manage their debt for a fee. They may ask for upfront payments or personal information, promising to reduce or eliminate student loans. In reality, these services are often available for free through legitimate government programs, and the scammer simply takes the money and disappears.

Scholarship scams involve fraudulent organizations offering fake scholarships to students. These scams often require an application fee or personal information. Once the fee is paid, the scholarship either never materializes, or the scammer uses the personal information for identity theft.

Employment scams target students seeking part-time jobs or internships. Scammers post fake job listings on online job boards, social media, or even through university career services. They may ask for personal information, such as Social Security numbers or bank account details, under the guise of processing payroll. In some cases, they send fake checks, asking the student to deposit the check and return a portion of the money. The check eventually bounces, leaving the student responsible for the funds.

Textbook scams exploit the high cost of educational materials. Scammers create fake websites or listings offering textbooks at significantly reduced prices. Students who purchase from these sources often receive counterfeit or no books at all, losing their money in the process.

Phishing attacks also target students. These attacks often come in the form of emails that appear to be from the university, financial aid office, or other trusted sources. The emails may ask students to verify their account information, update their passwords, or provide personal details. Clicking on the links or providing the requested information can result in stolen credentials and identity theft.

How to Protect Students from Scams

Protecting students from scams requires a combination of education, vigilance, and practical safeguards.

Financial Literacy Education: Educating students about financial management and the risks of scams is crucial. Universities and high schools can offer workshops, seminars, and online resources on topics such as budgeting, managing student loans, and recognizing fraud. Providing clear information about legitimate loan consolidation and forgiveness programs can help students avoid falling for scams.

Promoting Awareness of Common Scams: Universities and educational institutions should regularly inform students about common scams targeting their demographic. This can be done through email alerts, social media posts, and campus events. Highlighting recent scam trends and providing tips for avoiding fraud can keep students vigilant.

Encouraging Verification: Emphasize the importance of verifying any unsolicited offers, job postings, or scholarship opportunities. Students should contact the organization or individual directly using known contact information to confirm the legitimacy of the offer. Providing a list of trusted contacts and resources can be helpful.

Implementing Security Measures: Encourage students to use strong, unique passwords for their online accounts and enable multi-factor authentication where available. Regularly updating software and using antivirus programs can help protect their devices from malware and phishing attacks.

Secure Online Transactions: Advise students to use secure payment methods when making online purchases, especially for textbooks and educational materials. Reputable online retailers and university bookstores should be the preferred sources for purchasing textbooks.

Support Services: Universities can provide support services for students who encounter scams. This includes offering guidance on how to report fraud, assisting with identity theft recovery, and providing access to financial counseling. Having dedicated staff or offices to handle these issues can make a significant difference.

Case Studies: Real-Life Examples of Scams Targeting Specific Groups

Examining real-life examples of scams can provide valuable insights into how these schemes operate and how individuals and businesses can protect themselves. These case studies highlight the importance of vigilance, verification, and education in preventing fraud.

Case Study 1: The Grandparent Scam

Martha, an 82-year-old widow, received a phone call from someone claiming to be her grandson, Jake. The caller explained that he was traveling in Mexico, had been arrested, and needed $3,000 for bail. He pleaded with Martha not to tell his parents, as he was embarrassed and didn't want to worry them.

Concerned for her grandson, Martha went to her bank and wired the money to the account provided by the caller. Later that day, she mentioned the situation to her daughter, who immediately called Jake. Jake was safe at home and unaware of the call. Realizing she had been scammed, Martha reported the incident to her local police and the bank.

Analysis and Prevention:

- **What Went Wrong**: Martha was emotionally manipulated and acted quickly without verifying the caller's identity.

- **How It Could Have Been Avoided**: Martha could have avoided the scam by asking the caller specific questions that only her real grandson would know the answers to. She could also have contacted other family members to verify the situation before taking action.

Case Study 2: Business Email Compromise (BEC) Scam

A small manufacturing company, XYZ Corp, experienced a BEC scam when their CFO, John, received an urgent email from the CEO, requesting an immediate wire transfer of $50,000 to a new supplier. The email appeared legitimate, with the correct email address and company logo. Trusting the request, John authorized the transfer.

A few days later, the real CEO asked John about the payment, and they discovered that the CEO's email had been compromised. The scammer had gained access to the CEO's email account and sent the fraudulent request. XYZ Corp reported the incident to the FBI and their bank, but the chances of recovering the funds were slim.

Analysis and Prevention:

- **What Went Wrong**: John acted on the email request without verifying its authenticity, relying solely on the appearance of the email.

- **How It Could Have Been Avoided**: XYZ Corp could have implemented a protocol requiring multiple levels of approval for large transactions. John could have verified the request by calling the CEO directly or using a secondary communication channel.

Case Study 3: Student Loan Scam

Sarah, a college student, received a call from a company claiming to offer loan consolidation services. The representative explained that they could significantly reduce her monthly payments and eventually forgive her student loans. To proceed, Sarah needed to provide her Social Security number, loan details, and pay an upfront fee of $500.

Eager to reduce her debt, Sarah provided the requested information and paid the fee. Months later, she realized that her loan payments had not changed, and the company had disappeared. She contacted her loan servicer and learned that she had been scammed.

Analysis and Prevention:

- **What Went Wrong**: Sarah trusted the unsolicited call and provided sensitive information without verifying the company's legitimacy.

- **How It Could Have Been Avoided**: Sarah could have avoided the scam by researching the company and contacting her loan servicer directly to inquire about legitimate loan consolidation options. She should have been wary of upfront fees and verified the company's credentials.

Building Awareness and Resilience

Building awareness and resilience against scams targeting specific groups involves continuous education, proactive measures, and community support.

Education and Training: Regularly update educational materials and training programs to reflect the latest scam tactics. Schools, businesses, and community organizations can play a pivotal role in disseminating this information.

Community Support: Foster a sense of community where individuals feel comfortable discussing potential scams and seeking advice. Support networks can provide valuable insights and help prevent fraud.

Proactive Measures: Implement proactive measures such as account alerts, multi-factor authentication, and verification protocols. Regularly review and update these measures to ensure they remain effective.

Staying Informed: Keep up with the latest news and developments in fraud prevention. Government agencies, consumer protection organizations, and cybersecurity experts provide valuable resources and updates.

Institutional and Community Efforts

While individual actions are crucial, institutional and community efforts play a significant role in combating scams and supporting victims.

Businesses: Improve security practices and educate employees and customers about common scams. Providing clear communication about company policies can help prevent fraud. Offering resources and tools for account security can enhance protection.

Educational Institutions: Provide students with resources and support for managing their finances and recognizing scams. Financial literacy programs and workshops can help students make informed decisions.

Government Agencies: Regulate and enforce consumer protection laws. Investigating scams and prosecuting scammers are essential functions. Leading public awareness campaigns can educate the public about common scams and how to avoid them.

Community Organizations: Collaborate with government agencies and businesses to raise awareness about scams targeting specific groups. Hosting events and providing resources can empower individuals to protect themselves.

International Collaboration: Enhance efforts to combat cross-border scams. Information sharing, joint investigations, and coordinated enforcement actions can address global fraud.

Future Trends and Challenges

As technology evolves, so do the tactics and methods of scammers. Anticipating future trends in scams can help individuals and institutions stay ahead of emerging threats.

Artificial Intelligence (AI) and Machine Learning: Cybercriminals are likely to leverage AI to create more sophisticated scams. Personalized phishing emails and deepfake technology can make scams more convincing.

Cybersecurity Advancements: Developing advanced security technologies such as biometric authentication and blockchain can enhance protection. However, cybercriminals will continue to adapt, necessitating ongoing vigilance.

Global Collaboration: Combating global scams requires international cooperation. Information sharing and joint investigations are essential for addressing cross-border fraud.

Public Awareness and Education: Continuous efforts to educate the public about emerging scams are necessary. Leveraging digital platforms and social media can enhance the effectiveness of awareness campaigns.

Scams targeting specific groups, such as the elderly, businesses, and students, exploit unique vulnerabilities and circumstances. By understanding these scams and implementing protective measures, individuals and organizations can build a robust defense against fraud.

Individual actions, such as staying informed, using secure payment methods, and verifying requests, are crucial for preventing scams. Institutional and community efforts, including education, support networks, and regulatory measures, play a significant role in creating a safer environment.

Anticipating future trends and challenges in scams can help individuals and institutions stay ahead of emerging threats. By fostering a culture of awareness, vigilance, and resilience, we can protect ourselves and our communities from the harmful consequences of scams.

CHAPTER 8
INTERNATIONAL
SCAMS

In an increasingly interconnected world, international scams have become more prevalent and sophisticated, targeting individuals and businesses across borders. Understanding the nuances of global scams, recognizing the tactics used in different countries, and knowing how to protect yourself when traveling abroad are crucial in safeguarding against these threats. This chapter delves into the nature of international scams, offers insights into country-specific tactics, discusses common travel scams, and provides strategies for protecting yourself when traveling.

Global Scams

International scams encompass a wide range of fraudulent activities conducted by perpetrators from various countries. These scams often exploit the anonymity and reach of the internet, enabling scammers to target victims worldwide. The complexity and scale of these operations can make them challenging to detect and combat.

Common Types of Global Scams

One of the most pervasive global scams is the **advance-fee scam**. This scam typically involves a promise of a significant sum of money, such as an inheritance, lottery winnings, or business opportunity, in exchange for an upfront fee. The scammer may pose as a foreign official, businessperson, or attorney, requesting payment for administrative fees, taxes, or legal costs before the funds can be released. Victims who pay the fee never receive the promised money, and the scammer disappears.

Romance scams are also prevalent on a global scale. Scammers create fake profiles on dating sites or social media platforms, targeting individuals seeking companionship. They establish an emotional connection with the victim, often claiming to be from a different country. Eventually, the scammer fabricates a crisis, such as a medical emergency or travel mishap, and requests financial assistance. The victim, motivated by love and concern, sends money to the scammer, who continues to invent new reasons for needing funds until the victim realizes they have been duped.

Phishing scams are another common form of international fraud. Scammers send emails or messages that appear to be from reputable organizations, such as banks, government agencies, or well-known companies, asking the recipient to provide personal information or click on a malicious link. These scams can lead to identity theft, financial loss, and malware infections.

Lottery and sweepstakes scams target victims globally, often through unsolicited emails or letters claiming that the recipient has won a large prize. To claim the winnings, the victim is asked to pay fees or provide personal information. These scams prey on the excitement and hope of unexpected wealth, leading victims to comply with the scammer's demands.

Business email compromise (BEC) scams affect companies around the world. In this type of scam, cybercriminals gain access to a company's email system and send fraudulent messages to employees, customers, or partners, requesting payments or sensitive information. These scams can result in significant financial losses and damage to the company's reputation.

Understanding Scams from Different Countries

Scammers in different countries often employ tactics tailored to their local context and the cultural characteristics of their targets. Understanding these nuances can help individuals recognize and avoid international scams.

Nigerian Scams

Nigerian scammers, often associated with advance-fee fraud, use various tactics to lure victims. One of the most infamous scams is the "Nigerian Prince" scam, where the scammer claims to be a member of a royal family or a government official in need of assistance to transfer a large sum of money out of the country. The victim is promised a generous reward for their help but must first pay fees for legal documents or other expenses. Despite widespread awareness of this scam, it continues to be successful due to its emotional appeal and the promise of substantial rewards.

Indian Tech Support Scams

Tech support scams originating from India involve scammers posing as technicians from well-known technology companies, such as Microsoft or Apple. They contact victims, often in English-speaking countries, claiming that their computer is infected with malware or has a critical security issue. The scammer then offers to fix the problem for a fee or by gaining remote access to the victim's computer. This access allows the scammer to steal personal information, install malware, or charge for unnecessary services.

Chinese Phishing Scams

Phishing scams from China often target businesses and individuals with connections to Chinese companies or markets. These scams may involve emails that appear to be from legitimate Chinese businesses, requesting payments, sensitive information, or confirmation of financial transactions. The emails are typically well-crafted and may use company logos and professional language to appear credible. Scammers may also pose as suppliers or partners, tricking businesses into transferring funds to fraudulent accounts.

Russian Malware and Ransomware Attacks

Cybercriminals in Russia are known for sophisticated malware and ransomware attacks. These scams often involve phishing emails that deliver malicious software designed to encrypt the victim's files. The scammer then demands a ransom, typically in cryptocurrency, to restore access to the data. These attacks can target individuals, businesses, and even government agencies, causing significant disruption and financial loss.

Brazilian Banking Scams

In Brazil, banking scams are prevalent, with scammers using techniques such as phishing, vishing (voice phishing), and smishing (SMS phishing) to steal banking credentials and financial information. These scams often involve fake emails, phone calls, or text messages that appear to be from legitimate banks, asking the victim to verify their account information or reset their password. Once the scammer obtains the credentials, they can access the victim's bank account and steal funds.

Travel Scams

Travel scams target tourists and travelers, exploiting their unfamiliarity with local customs, languages, and environments. These scams can occur at various stages of a trip, from planning and booking to navigating foreign cities. Being aware of common travel scams and knowing how to protect yourself can help ensure a safe and enjoyable journey.

Booking Scams

Booking scams involve fraudulent websites or agencies offering discounted travel deals, including flights, hotels, and vacation packages. Victims who book through these channels may find that their reservations do not exist, the accommodations are subpar, or the agency disappears after taking payment. To avoid booking scams, always use reputable travel agencies and websites, verify reviews and ratings, and pay with a credit card, which offers better fraud protection.

Taxi and Transportation Scams

Taxi scams are common in many tourist destinations. Drivers may overcharge by taking longer routes, using rigged meters, or quoting inflated fares. In some cases, drivers may claim that a hotel or attraction is closed and offer to take the passenger to a different location where they receive a commission. To protect yourself, use official taxi services, agree on the fare before the ride, or use ride-hailing apps with transparent pricing.

Fake Tour Guides and Tickets

Scammers may pose as official tour guides, offering services at popular tourist attractions. These fake guides may provide misleading or incorrect information, overcharge for their services, or take tourists to shops where they receive kickbacks.

Similarly, fake tickets to attractions or events may be sold at inflated prices or be completely worthless. To avoid these scams, book tours and tickets through reputable sources and verify the credentials of guides and sellers.

Pickpocketing and Distraction Scams

Pickpocketing is a common threat in crowded tourist areas, with scammers using various distraction techniques to steal wallets, phones, and other valuables. These techniques may include spilling something on the victim, causing a commotion, or engaging in close physical contact. To protect yourself, keep your belongings secure, use anti-theft bags, and be aware of your surroundings. Avoid carrying large amounts of cash and store important documents in a hotel safe.

Fake Police Officers

In some countries, scammers pose as police officers and approach tourists, claiming that they need to check their identification or search their belongings for counterfeit currency or drugs. The fake officers may then steal money or valuables during the search. To protect yourself, always ask for identification and verify the authenticity of the officers. If in doubt, offer to go to the nearest police station to resolve the issue.

Currency Exchange Scams

Currency exchange scams can occur at unofficial exchange booths or with individuals offering to exchange money on the street. These scammers may use inflated exchange rates, charge hidden fees, or provide counterfeit currency. To avoid these scams, use official exchange services at banks, airports, or reputable exchange bureaus. Familiarize yourself with the current exchange rates and calculate the expected amount before making the exchange.

Accommodation Scams

Accommodation scams involve fraudulent listings on booking platforms or classifieds websites. Scammers may advertise non-existent properties, use photos of legitimate properties without permission, or list properties they do not own. Victims who book these accommodations may arrive to find that the property does not exist or is already occupied. To protect yourself, use reputable booking platforms, read reviews, and communicate directly with the property owner or manager before making a payment.

Protecting Yourself When Traveling Abroad

Traveling abroad can be an enriching experience, but it also requires heightened awareness and precautionary measures to protect against scams. Here are some strategies to safeguard yourself and your belongings when traveling internationally.

Research Your Destination

Before traveling, research your destination thoroughly. Understand the common scams in the area, local customs, and any specific safety concerns. Travel forums, guidebooks, and government travel advisories can provide valuable insights. Being well-informed about potential risks can help you stay vigilant and avoid falling victim to scams.

Use Reputable Services

When booking flights, accommodations, tours, and transportation, use reputable and well-reviewed services. Trusted travel agencies, official websites, and established platforms offer better protection against fraud. Verify the legitimacy of services through reviews, ratings, and recommendations from fellow travelers.

Secure Your Belongings

Keep your belongings secure by using anti-theft bags, money belts, and secure pockets. Avoid displaying expensive items, such as jewelry or electronics, which can attract attention. Store important documents, such as passports and travel insurance, in a hotel safe or another secure location. Make copies of essential documents and keep them separate from the originals.

Stay Connected

Stay connected with friends and family during your trip. Share your itinerary and check in regularly to keep them informed of your whereabouts. In case of an emergency, having someone who knows your plans can be crucial. Consider using a local SIM card or an international phone plan to ensure you have reliable communication.

Be Cautious with Public Wi-Fi

Public Wi-Fi networks can be vulnerable to cyberattacks, making it easy for scammers to intercept your data. Avoid accessing sensitive information, such as banking or personal accounts, over public Wi-Fi. Use a virtual private network (VPN) to encrypt your internet connection and protect your data from eavesdropping.

Verify Credentials

When dealing with authorities, tour guides, or service providers, always verify their credentials. Official personnel should carry identification, and legitimate services should provide proof of authorization. If you are unsure, seek confirmation through trusted sources or contact the relevant authorities directly.

Keep Emergency Contacts Handy

Have a list of emergency contacts, including local police, your country's embassy or consulate, and emergency services. In case of a scam or any other emergency, knowing who to contact can help you quickly address the situation and seek assistance.

Avoid Over-Sharing

Be cautious about sharing personal information with strangers. Scammers may use seemingly innocent conversations to gather details about you and exploit them. Protect your privacy by limiting the amount of personal information you disclose.

Trust Your Instincts

If something feels off or too good to be true, trust your instincts. Scammers often rely on creating a sense of urgency or excitement to cloud your judgment. Taking a moment to assess the situation critically can help you avoid falling victim to fraud.

Know Your Rights

Familiarize yourself with your rights as a traveler, including consumer protection laws and procedures for reporting scams. Knowing your rights can empower you to take appropriate action if you encounter a fraudulent situation.

Use Credit Cards for Transactions

Using credit cards for transactions provides better protection against fraud compared to cash or debit cards. Credit card companies often offer fraud detection services and may reimburse unauthorized charges. Notify your credit card provider of your travel plans to avoid any issues with international transactions.

Case Studies: International Scams

Examining real-life case studies of international scams can provide valuable insights into how these schemes operate and how travelers can protect themselves.

Case Study 1: The Nigerian Prince Scam

John, an American businessman, received an email from someone claiming to be Prince Adebayo of Nigeria. The email explained that the prince needed assistance in transferring $20 million out of the country and offered John a 10% commission for his help. To facilitate the transfer, John was asked to pay $5,000 in administrative fees.

Tempted by the prospect of a substantial reward, John wired the money. Over the next few weeks, the prince requested additional payments for various expenses. John eventually realized that he had been scammed and reported the incident to the authorities, but the chances of recovering his money were slim.

Analysis and Prevention:

- **What Went Wrong**: John was lured by the promise of easy money and did not verify the legitimacy of the request.

- **How It Could Have Been Avoided**: John could have avoided the scam by recognizing the red flags associated with advance-fee scams. Verifying the request through independent research and consulting with trusted individuals could have prevented him from falling victim.

Case Study 2: The Indian Tech Support Scam

Linda, a retiree in Canada, received a call from someone claiming to be a technician from Microsoft. The caller informed Linda that her computer was infected with a virus and needed immediate attention. He instructed her to download a remote access tool so he could fix the issue.

Concerned about her computer's security, Linda followed the instructions. The scammer then gained access to her computer, installed malware, and charged her $300 for the "service." Linda's personal information was also compromised, leading to further financial losses.

Analysis and Prevention:

- **What Went Wrong**: Linda trusted the unsolicited call and allowed the scammer to access her computer without verifying his credentials.

- **How It Could Have Been Avoided**: Linda could have avoided the scam by being skeptical of unsolicited tech support calls. Contacting Microsoft directly through their official support channels and using reputable antivirus software could have protected her computer and personal information.

Case Study 3: The Chinese Phishing Scam

Michael, a manager at a logistics company in the United States, received an email that appeared to be from a supplier in China. The email requested payment for an outstanding invoice and included updated bank account details. The email looked legitimate, with the supplier's logo and professional language.

Trusting the email, Michael authorized the payment. A few

days later, the real supplier contacted him, inquiring about the overdue payment. Michael realized that he had transferred the funds to a scammer's account and reported the incident to his bank and the authorities.

Analysis and Prevention:

- **What Went Wrong**: Michael trusted the email without verifying the updated payment details with the supplier.

- **How It Could Have Been Avoided**: Michael could have avoided the scam by implementing a verification process for any changes in payment instructions. Contacting the supplier directly through known contact information to confirm the request could have prevented the fraudulent transfer.

Building Awareness and Resilience

Building awareness and resilience against international scams involves continuous education, vigilance, and the implementation of proactive measures.

Education and Training: Regularly update educational materials and training programs to reflect the latest scam tactics. Travel agencies, businesses, and community organizations can play a pivotal role in disseminating this information.

Community Support: Foster a sense of community where individuals feel comfortable discussing potential scams and seeking advice. Support networks can provide valuable insights and help prevent fraud.

Proactive Measures: Implement proactive measures such as account alerts, multi-factor authentication, and verification protocols. Regularly review and update these measures to ensure they remain effective.

Staying Informed: Keep up with the latest news and developments in fraud prevention. Government agencies, consumer protection organizations, and cybersecurity experts provide valuable resources and updates.

Institutional and Community Efforts

While individual actions are crucial, institutional and community efforts play a significant role in combating international scams and supporting victims.

Businesses: Improve security practices and educate employees and customers about common international scams. Providing clear communication about company policies can help prevent fraud. Offering resources and tools for account security can enhance protection.

Travel Agencies and Tourism Boards: Provide travelers with resources and support for recognizing and avoiding scams. Offering guidance on safe travel practices and distributing informational materials can help tourists protect themselves.

Government Agencies: Regulate and enforce consumer protection laws. Investigating scams and prosecuting scammers are essential functions. Leading public awareness campaigns can educate the public about common scams and how to avoid them.

Community Organizations: Collaborate with government agencies and businesses to raise awareness about international scams. Hosting events and providing resources can empower individuals to protect themselves.

International Collaboration: Enhance efforts to combat cross-border scams. Information sharing, joint investigations, and coordinated enforcement actions can address global fraud.

Future Trends and Challenges

As technology evolves, so do the tactics and methods of scammers. Anticipating future trends in international scams can help individuals and institutions stay ahead of emerging threats.

Artificial Intelligence (AI) and Machine Learning: Cybercriminals are likely to leverage AI to create more sophisticated scams. Personalized phishing emails and deepfake technology can make scams more convincing.

Cybersecurity Advancements: Developing advanced security technologies such as biometric authentication and blockchain can enhance protection. However, cybercriminals will continue to adapt, necessitating ongoing vigilance.

Global Collaboration: Combating global scams requires international cooperation. Information sharing and joint investigations are essential for addressing cross-border fraud.

Public Awareness and Education: Continuous efforts to educate the public about emerging scams are necessary. Leveraging digital platforms and social media can enhance the effectiveness of awareness campaigns.

CHAPTER 9 RESOURCES AND HELP

When facing the threat or aftermath of scams, having access to reliable resources and support networks is crucial. This chapter provides a comprehensive guide to support networks, organizations, hotlines, educational resources, websites, books, courses, and a bibliography for further reading. By leveraging these resources, individuals and businesses can better protect themselves against scams and find assistance if they become victims.

Support Networks

Support networks play a vital role in helping individuals and businesses cope with the emotional and financial impacts of scams. These networks can provide guidance, share experiences, and offer practical advice.

Family and Friends

One of the most immediate and accessible support networks is your circle of family and friends. These trusted individuals can offer emotional support and practical assistance, such as helping to monitor accounts, report scams, or provide transportation to meetings with law enforcement or financial institutions. Sharing your experiences with them can also raise awareness and prevent them from becoming victims of similar scams.

Community Groups

Community groups, including local clubs, senior centers, and neighborhood associations, can provide a sense of solidarity and collective vigilance against scams. Many community groups hold informational sessions and workshops on fraud prevention, offering a platform for members to share their experiences and learn from each other. Joining such groups can help you stay informed about local scam trends and protective measures.

Online Forums and Social Media Groups

The internet offers numerous online forums and social media groups dedicated to discussing scams and fraud prevention. Platforms like Reddit, Facebook, and specialized forums such as Scamwatcher allow users to share their experiences, ask questions, and receive advice from a global community. These online communities can be valuable resources for staying updated on the latest scam tactics and finding support from others who have been through similar experiences.

Organizations and Hotlines

Various organizations and hotlines provide specialized support for scam victims, offering assistance with reporting fraud, recovering losses, and accessing legal resources.

Federal Trade Commission (FTC)

The FTC is a leading agency in the fight against consumer fraud in the United States. It provides extensive resources for scam prevention and recovery, including a dedicated website for reporting scams (ftc.gov/complaint). The FTC also publishes educational materials and conducts public awareness campaigns to help consumers recognize and avoid scams.

Internet Crime Complaint Center (IC3)

Operated by the FBI, the IC3 is a central hub for reporting internet-based crimes, including scams. Victims can file complaints through the IC3 website (ic3.gov), which helps federal law enforcement agencies track and investigate online fraud. The IC3 also provides guidance on how to protect yourself from cybercrime and what to do if you become a victim.

Better Business Bureau (BBB)

The BBB helps consumers find trustworthy businesses and avoid scams. It offers a platform for reporting and resolving complaints against businesses, as well as a scam tracker tool that maps reported scams across North America. The BBB's website (bbb.org) features tips and resources for recognizing and avoiding fraud.

National Fraud Information Center (NFIC)

The NFIC, run by the National Consumers League, provides information and resources on various types of fraud, including internet, telemarketing, and charity scams. Victims can call the NFIC hotline (800-876-7060) to report scams and receive advice on how to handle fraudulent situations.

AARP Fraud Watch Network

AARP's Fraud Watch Network is a valuable resource for older adults, providing tools and resources to protect against scams. It offers a helpline (877-908-3360) where individuals can report scams and receive support from trained fraud specialists. The

Fraud Watch Network also features educational content and alerts about emerging scam trends.

Consumer Financial Protection Bureau (CFPB)

The CFPB focuses on protecting consumers in the financial sector. It offers resources on preventing financial scams, managing debt, and reporting fraudulent activities. The CFPB's website (consumerfinance.gov) includes a section dedicated to scams and fraud, providing valuable information and support.

Identity Theft Resource Center (ITRC)

The ITRC is a non-profit organization that provides assistance to victims of identity theft and data breaches. Its services include a toll-free hotline (888-400-5530), educational resources, and personalized support for resolving identity theft issues. The ITRC's website (idtheftcenter.org) offers tools and information on how to protect your identity and recover from identity theft.

Educational Resources

Education is a powerful tool in the fight against scams. Numerous resources are available to help individuals and businesses learn about fraud prevention and protection strategies.

Websites

- **Scamwatch (scamwatch.gov.au)**: Run by the Australian Competition and Consumer Commission (ACCC), Scamwatch provides information on how to recognize, avoid, and report scams. It features a comprehensive database of scam types, real-life examples, and advice on what to do if you become a victim.

- **OnGuardOnline (onguardonline.gov)**: Managed by the FTC, OnGuardOnline offers practical tips and resources for staying safe online. The website covers topics such as phishing, identity theft, and online shopping security, providing tools and quizzes to test your knowledge.

- **Action Fraud (actionfraud.police.uk)**: The UK's national reporting center for fraud and cybercrime, Action Fraud provides a platform for reporting scams and accessing support. The website includes educational content on various types of fraud and advice on how to protect yourself.

- **Stay Safe Online (staysafeonline.org)**: An initiative of the National Cyber Security Alliance, Stay Safe Online offers resources for individuals and businesses to improve their cybersecurity practices. The website covers topics such as safe browsing, password management, and protecting personal information.

Books

- **"Scam Me If You Can: Simple Strategies to Outsmart Today's Rip-off Artists" by Frank Abagnale**: Written by a former con artist turned security consultant, this book offers insights into common scams and practical advice on how to avoid them. Abagnale shares his expertise on recognizing fraud and protecting yourself from various types of scams.

- **"The Art of Deception: Controlling the Human Element of Security" by Kevin D. Mitnick**: This book explores the techniques used by social engineers to manipulate individuals and gain access to sensitive information. Mitnick, a former hacker, provides valuable insights into how scammers exploit human vulnerabilities and offers strategies for protecting against such attacks.

- **"Identity Theft Alert: 10 Rules You Must Follow to Protect Yourself from America's #1 Crime" by Steve Weisman**: Weisman, a legal expert, outlines key steps to protect against identity theft. The book covers various forms of identity theft, including online and offline tactics, and provides practical tips for safeguarding personal information.

Courses

- **Coursera's "Cybersecurity Specialization"**: Offered by the University of Maryland, this specialization covers fundamental concepts of cybersecurity, including network security, cryptography, and secure coding practices. The courses provide a solid foundation for understanding and protecting against cyber threats.

- **edX's "Introduction to Cyber Security"**: Provided by the University of Washington, this course offers an overview of cybersecurity principles and practices. It covers topics such as threat analysis, risk management, and incident response, helping learners develop essential skills for protecting against cybercrime.

- **Udemy's "Cyber Security Awareness: Security Training for the Workplace"**: This course is designed to educate employees on common cyber threats and best practices for maintaining security in the workplace. It covers topics such as phishing, password management, and safe internet usage.

Comprehensive List of References and Further Reading Materials

Having access to a well-rounded collection of references and further reading materials can enhance your understanding of scams and fraud prevention. Here is a comprehensive list of recommended resources:

Websites

- **Federal Trade Commission (ftc.gov)**: The FTC offers extensive resources on consumer protection, including information on common scams, identity theft, and how to report fraud.

- **Better Business Bureau (bbb.org)**: The BBB provides a scam tracker tool, consumer reviews, and tips for avoiding fraud.

- **Internet Crime Complaint Center (ic3.gov)**: The IC3 is the FBI's platform for reporting internet-based crimes, offering resources on cybercrime prevention and recovery.

- **AARP Fraud Watch Network (aarp.org/fraudwatchnetwork)**: AARP provides tools and resources specifically for older adults, including a helpline and educational content on scam prevention.

Books

- **"Swiped: How to Protect Yourself in a World Full of Scammers, Phishers, and Identity Thieves" by Adam Levin**: This book offers practical advice on protecting personal information and preventing identity theft. Levin shares real-life stories and provides actionable steps for safeguarding against fraud.

- **"Cybersecurity for Dummies" by Joseph Steinberg**: A comprehensive guide to understanding and implementing cybersecurity practices, this book covers topics such as data protection, threat detection, and safe internet usage.

- **"Data and Goliath: The Hidden Battles to Collect Your Data and Control Your World" by Bruce Schneier**: Schneier, a renowned security expert, explores the implications of data collection and surveillance, providing insights into how individuals can protect their privacy.

Courses

- **LinkedIn Learning's "Learning Cyber Security"**: This course provides an introduction to cybersecurity concepts, including threat landscapes, security frameworks, and best practices for protecting personal and organizational data.

- **FutureLearn's "Introduction to Cyber Security"**: Offered by The Open University, this course covers the basics of cybersecurity, including threat identification, risk management, and incident response.

- **Khan Academy's "Internet Safety"**: A free course that covers fundamental principles of online safety, including protecting personal information, recognizing scams, and using secure passwords.

Building Awareness and Resilience

Building awareness and resilience against scams requires

a proactive approach, leveraging available resources, and fostering a culture of vigilance and continuous learning.

Continuous Education

Stay updated on the latest scam trends and prevention strategies by regularly accessing educational resources, attending workshops, and participating in online courses. Many organizations and educational institutions offer free or low-cost training programs that can help you stay informed and prepared.

Community Engagement

Engage with your community through local events, online forums, and social media groups dedicated to scam prevention. Sharing your experiences and learning from others can enhance your understanding of scams and how to avoid them.

Proactive Measures

Implement proactive measures such as using strong passwords, enabling multi-factor authentication, and monitoring your accounts for unusual activity. Regularly review and update your security practices to ensure they remain effective.

Institutional Support

Encourage businesses and organizations to prioritize security and provide resources for employees and customers. Clear communication about company policies, regular training sessions, and access to support services can help create a safer environment.

Institutional and Community Efforts

While individual actions are crucial, institutional and community efforts play a significant role in combating scams and supporting victims.

Government Agencies

Government agencies should continue to regulate and enforce consumer protection laws, investigate scams, and prosecute scammers. Leading public awareness campaigns and providing resources for scam prevention are essential functions.

Businesses

Businesses can improve their security practices and educate employees and customers about common scams. Offering resources and tools for account security, conducting regular training sessions, and maintaining clear communication about company policies can help prevent fraud.

Community Organizations

Community organizations can collaborate with government agencies and businesses to raise awareness about scams. Hosting events, providing informational materials, and offering support services can empower individuals to protect themselves.

International Collaboration

International collaboration is increasingly important in combating global scams. Information sharing, joint investigations, and coordinated enforcement actions can enhance efforts to address cross-border fraud.

Future Trends and Challenges

As technology evolves, so do the tactics and methods of scammers. Anticipating future trends in scams can help individuals and institutions stay ahead of emerging threats.

Artificial Intelligence (AI) and Machine Learning

Cybercriminals are likely to leverage AI and machine learning to create more sophisticated scams. Personalized phishing emails, deepfake technology, and automated attacks can make scams more convincing and difficult to detect.

Cybersecurity Advancements

Developing advanced security technologies, such as biometric authentication and blockchain, can enhance protection against scams. However, cybercriminals will continue to adapt, necessitating ongoing vigilance and innovation.

Global Collaboration

Combating global scams requires international cooperation. Information sharing, joint investigations, and coordinated enforcement actions are essential for addressing cross-border fraud.

Public Awareness and Education

Continuous efforts to educate the public about emerging scams are necessary. Leveraging digital platforms and social media can enhance the effectiveness of awareness campaigns and reach a broader audience.

CHAPTER 10
TECHNOLOGICAL
ADVANCES AND SCAMS

As technology continues to evolve at an unprecedented pace, so too do the tactics employed by scammers. In this chapter, we will explore how technological advances such as artificial intelligence, cryptocurrency, and deepfake technology have transformed the landscape of scams. Understanding these developments is crucial for recognizing and mitigating the risks associated with modern fraud. We will delve into how AI is used in scams, the specific nature of cryptocurrency fraud, the threats posed by deepfakes, and other new technologies that scammers are leveraging.

Artificial Intelligence and Scams

Artificial intelligence (AI) is a double-edged sword in the realm of cybersecurity. While it offers powerful tools for detecting and preventing scams, it also provides scammers with sophisticated methods to execute their schemes more effectively.

How AI is Used in Scams

AI has enabled scammers to create more personalized and convincing fraudulent schemes. One of the primary ways AI is used in scams is through **phishing attacks**. Traditional phishing emails often rely on generic content that can be easily identified as spam. However, AI allows scammers to analyze vast amounts of data and generate personalized phishing emails that are tailored to the specific interests and behaviors of their targets. This level of customization increases the likelihood of the victim falling for the scam.

Another application of AI in scams is through **chatbots**. Scammers deploy AI-driven chatbots on social media platforms, dating sites, and customer service portals to interact with potential victims. These chatbots can engage in realistic conversations, build trust, and eventually steer the conversation towards fraudulent schemes. For example, a chatbot on a dating site might develop a romantic relationship with a victim before requesting money for a fabricated emergency.

Social engineering is another area where AI has made scams more effective. AI can analyze social media profiles, public records, and other online information to build detailed profiles of potential victims. Scammers can use this information to craft highly convincing narratives that exploit the victim's specific circumstances, such as impersonating a trusted contact or referencing personal details that lend credibility to the scam.

Voice synthesis technology, powered by AI, has also become a tool for scammers. By analyzing voice recordings, AI can generate synthetic voices that mimic the sound of a specific individual. This technology enables scammers to conduct **vishing** (voice phishing) attacks, where they impersonate someone the victim knows and trusts, such as a family member, colleague, or authority figure, to extract sensitive information or money.

How AI Can Help Prevent Scams

Despite its use in scams, AI is also a powerful tool in the fight against fraud. One of the key ways AI can help prevent scams is through **anomaly detection**. AI algorithms can analyze patterns in financial transactions, communication logs, and other data streams to identify deviations from the norm. These anomalies can signal potential fraudulent activity, allowing for early intervention and prevention.

Natural language processing (NLP), a subset of AI, can be used to analyze text and identify characteristics of phishing emails or fraudulent messages. By examining language patterns, word choices, and contextual clues, NLP algorithms can flag suspicious communications before they reach the intended target.

Behavioral biometrics is another area where AI is making strides in fraud prevention. This technology analyzes the unique ways individuals interact with their devices, such as typing rhythms, mouse movements, and touchscreen behavior. By establishing a behavioral baseline, AI can detect deviations that may indicate unauthorized access or fraudulent activity, prompting additional security measures.

AI-driven **fraud detection systems** are increasingly being integrated into financial institutions and online platforms. These systems continuously monitor transactions and user activities, leveraging machine learning algorithms to detect and block suspicious behavior in real time. As these systems learn from new data, they become more adept at identifying and thwarting emerging scam tactics.

Cryptocurrency Scams

Cryptocurrency, with its decentralized and anonymous nature, has become both an innovative financial instrument and a fertile ground for scammers. Understanding the specific nature of cryptocurrency fraud and implementing protection measures is essential for anyone involved in the digital currency space.

Understanding Crypto-Specific Fraud

Cryptocurrency scams come in various forms, each exploiting the unique features of digital currencies. One common type is the **investment scam**, where scammers create fake cryptocurrency investment platforms or initial coin offerings (ICOs). They promise high returns and use sophisticated marketing tactics to attract investors. Once they collect a significant amount of money, the scammers disappear, leaving investors with worthless tokens.

Phishing attacks targeting cryptocurrency users are also prevalent. Scammers send emails or messages that appear to be from legitimate cryptocurrency exchanges or wallet providers, prompting users to enter their login credentials on fake websites. Once the scammers obtain these credentials, they gain access to the victims' accounts and steal their funds.

Ponzi schemes and **pyramid schemes** have found a new life in the cryptocurrency world. Scammers promise high returns on cryptocurrency investments, which are paid out using the funds of new investors. These schemes collapse when there are not enough new investors to pay the earlier ones, resulting in significant losses for most participants.

Rug pulls are a type of scam associated with decentralized finance (DeFi) projects. In a rug pull, developers create a new cryptocurrency or DeFi project, attract investors, and then abruptly withdraw all the funds, leaving investors with worthless tokens. This scam exploits the lack of regulation and oversight in the DeFi space.

Cryptojacking is another crypto-specific fraud where scammers use malware to hijack a victim's computer or device to mine cryptocurrency without their knowledge. This type of scam can go unnoticed for a long time, as it does not directly steal funds but instead uses the victim's resources to generate cryptocurrency for the scammer.

Protection Measures

Protecting yourself from cryptocurrency scams involves a combination of vigilance, education, and the use of security tools. One of the most critical steps is to **conduct thorough research** before investing in any cryptocurrency or related project. Verify the legitimacy of the platform, review the project's whitepaper, check the credentials of the team members, and look for independent reviews and analyses.

Use reputable exchanges and wallets. Stick to well-known and established cryptocurrency exchanges and wallet providers with robust security measures and positive user feedback. Avoid using unknown or poorly reviewed services, especially those offering deals that seem too good to be true.

Enable two-factor authentication (2FA) on all cryptocurrency accounts. This adds an extra layer of security by requiring a second form of verification, such as a code sent to your mobile device, in addition to your password.

Be wary of unsolicited communications. Scammers often use phishing emails, messages, and social media posts to lure victims. Always verify the authenticity of any communication by contacting the company or individual directly through official channels.

Keep your software and devices updated. Ensure that your computer, mobile devices, and any cryptocurrency-related applications are up to date with the latest security patches and updates. This helps protect against vulnerabilities that scammers might exploit.

Store your cryptocurrency securely. Use hardware wallets or other secure storage solutions for holding significant amounts of cryptocurrency. Avoid keeping large sums on exchanges, which can be more susceptible to hacking.

Deepfakes and Impersonation

Deepfake technology, which uses AI to create hyper-realistic but fake videos and audio, presents a new frontier in the realm of scams. This technology can be used to create convincing impersonations, leading to a range of fraudulent activities.

Understanding Deepfakes

Deepfakes leverage machine learning techniques to manipulate videos and audio, making it appear as though a person is saying or doing something they never did. This technology can be used to create highly realistic videos of public figures, executives, or even personal acquaintances, making it challenging to distinguish between real and fake content.

Applications in Scams

Deepfakes can be used in **impersonation scams**, where scammers create fake videos or audio recordings of individuals in positions of authority to deceive victims. For example, a scammer might create a deepfake video of a company CEO instructing an employee to transfer funds to a fraudulent account. The realistic nature of the deepfake makes it highly convincing and increases the likelihood of compliance.

In **social engineering attacks**, deepfakes can be used to impersonate trusted individuals, such as family members or friends, to extract sensitive information or money. For instance, a scammer might create a deepfake audio message from a loved one requesting urgent financial assistance, prompting the victim to act without verifying the request.

Political and reputational attacks are another area where deepfakes pose significant risks. Scammers can create fake videos or audio recordings of public figures making controversial statements or engaging in inappropriate behavior. These deepfakes can be used to manipulate public opinion, damage reputations, or influence elections.

Protection Measures

Protecting against deepfake-related scams requires a combination of technological solutions and critical thinking. **Verification** is crucial. If you receive a request that seems unusual or out of character, verify it through multiple channels. For example, if you receive a video or audio message from a colleague asking for a sensitive action, contact them directly through a known phone number or in person to confirm the request.

Stay informed about the latest developments in deepfake technology and the methods used to create and detect them. Being aware of the potential risks can help you recognize suspicious content and take appropriate action.

Use deepfake detection tools. Several AI-driven tools and platforms are being developed to detect deepfake content. These tools analyze videos and audio for inconsistencies and signs of manipulation, helping to identify fraudulent content.

Educate and train employees and individuals on the risks associated with deepfakes and the importance of verification. Regular training sessions and informational materials can raise awareness and promote vigilance.

Advocate for regulatory measures. Encourage policymakers to develop and implement regulations that address the misuse of deepfake technology. Legal frameworks can help deter scammers and provide recourse for victims of deepfake-related fraud.

New Technologies Scammers Use

Beyond AI and deepfakes, scammers are continually adopting new technologies to enhance their schemes. Understanding these emerging tools can help individuals and businesses stay ahead of potential threats.

Internet of Things (IoT)

The proliferation of IoT devices, such as smart home systems, wearable technology, and connected appliances, has introduced new vulnerabilities. Scammers can exploit weak security in IoT devices to gain unauthorized access to networks, steal personal information, or launch attacks. For example, a compromised smart home device could be used to eavesdrop on conversations or manipulate home security systems.

Blockchain Technology

While blockchain is often touted for its security features, it is not immune to exploitation. Scammers have developed techniques to manipulate smart contracts, launch attacks on decentralized exchanges, and execute **pump-and-dump schemes**. These schemes involve artificially inflating the price of a cryptocurrency through false or misleading statements, then selling off the holdings at the peak, leaving other investors with worthless assets.

Augmented Reality (AR) and Virtual Reality (VR)

AR and VR technologies are becoming increasingly popular in gaming, education, and business. Scammers can create fake AR or VR environments to deceive users into providing personal information or making fraudulent transactions. For instance, a scammer might create a virtual storefront in a VR environment that mimics a legitimate business, tricking users into making purchases with real money.

Social Media Manipulation Tools

Scammers use advanced tools to create and manage fake social media profiles, automate interactions, and spread disinformation. These tools can amplify fraudulent campaigns, making them appear more credible and widespread. For example, a scammer might use social media manipulation tools to create the illusion of a popular investment opportunity, attracting unsuspecting victims.

Protection Measures

Protecting against scams that leverage new technologies requires a proactive and multifaceted approach.

Strengthen IoT security by changing default passwords,

regularly updating firmware, and using secure networks. Implementing network segmentation can also help isolate IoT devices from critical systems.

Be cautious with blockchain investments. Conduct thorough research, verify the legitimacy of projects, and be wary of schemes that promise high returns with little risk. Use reputable exchanges and wallets, and enable security features such as multi-factor authentication.

Verify AR and VR environments. Before making transactions or sharing personal information in AR or VR environments, verify the authenticity of the platform and the entities involved. Use secure payment methods and be cautious of deals that seem too good to be true.

Educate and train individuals on recognizing and avoiding social media manipulation. Encourage critical thinking and verification of information before taking action based on social media content. Use tools and services that detect and report fake profiles and disinformation campaigns.

Building Awareness and Resilience

Building awareness and resilience against technologically advanced scams involves continuous education, vigilance, and the implementation of proactive measures.

Continuous Education

Stay updated on the latest technological advancements and their implications for fraud. Access educational resources, attend workshops, and participate in online courses to stay informed and prepared.

Community Engagement

Engage with your community through local events, online forums, and social media groups dedicated to scam prevention. Sharing experiences and learning from others can enhance your understanding of emerging threats and protective measures.

Proactive Measures

Implement proactive measures such as using strong passwords, enabling multi-factor authentication, and regularly monitoring your accounts for unusual activity. Regularly review and update your security practices to ensure they remain effective.

Institutional Support

Encourage businesses and organizations to prioritize security and provide resources for employees and customers. Clear communication about company policies, regular training sessions, and access to support services can help create a safer environment.

Institutional and Community Efforts

While individual actions are crucial, institutional and community efforts play a significant role in combating technologically advanced scams and supporting victims.

Government Agencies

Government agencies should continue to regulate and enforce consumer protection laws, investigate scams, and prosecute scammers. Leading public awareness campaigns and providing resources for scam prevention are essential functions.

Businesses

Businesses can improve their security practices and educate employees and customers about common scams. Offering resources and tools for account security, conducting regular training sessions, and maintaining clear communication about company policies can help prevent fraud.

Community Organizations

Community organizations can collaborate with government agencies and businesses to raise awareness about scams. Hosting events, providing informational materials, and offering support services can empower individuals to protect themselves.

International Collaboration

International collaboration is increasingly important in combating global scams. Information sharing, joint investigations, and coordinated enforcement actions can enhance efforts to address cross-border fraud.

Future Trends and Challenges

As technology evolves, so do the tactics and methods of scammers. Anticipating future trends in technologically advanced scams can help individuals and institutions stay ahead of emerging threats.

Artificial Intelligence (AI) and Machine Learning

Cybercriminals are likely to continue leveraging AI and machine learning to create more sophisticated scams. Personalized phishing emails, deepfake technology, and automated attacks will become increasingly prevalent and challenging to detect.

Cybersecurity Advancements

Developing advanced security technologies, such as biometric authentication and blockchain, can enhance protection against scams. However, cybercriminals will continue to adapt, necessitating ongoing vigilance and innovation.

Global Collaboration

Combating global scams requires international cooperation. Information sharing, joint investigations, and coordinated enforcement actions are essential for addressing cross-border fraud.

Public Awareness and Education

Continuous efforts to educate the public about emerging scams are necessary. Leveraging digital platforms and social media can enhance the effectiveness of awareness campaigns and reach a broader audience.

CHAPTER 11
PSYCHOLOGICAL
RESILIENCE

Psychological resilience is the ability to adapt to adversity, stress, and trauma, emerging stronger and more capable of handling future challenges. For victims of scams, building resilience is essential for recovery and prevention of future incidents. This chapter explores the concept of resilience, techniques to strengthen mental fortitude, ways to deal with shame and guilt, coping strategies, the role of support groups, and finding emotional support and counseling services.

Building Resilience

Resilience is not an innate trait but a skill that can be developed over time. Building resilience involves adopting a mindset that embraces growth, learning from experiences, and maintaining a positive outlook despite hardships.

Adopt a Growth Mindset

A growth mindset is the belief that abilities and intelligence can be developed through effort, learning, and persistence. Embracing this mindset encourages individuals to see challenges as opportunities for growth rather than insurmountable obstacles. This perspective can be particularly empowering for scam victims, helping them to view the experience as a learning opportunity rather than a definitive failure.

Develop Emotional Awareness

Emotional awareness involves recognizing and understanding your emotions, which is crucial for managing stress and building resilience. Practicing mindfulness and self-reflection can enhance emotional awareness, allowing you to respond to challenges with greater clarity and composure. Techniques such as journaling, meditation, and mindfulness exercises can help you become more attuned to your emotional states.

Foster Strong Relationships

Building and maintaining strong relationships with family, friends, and community members provides a support network that can offer comfort, advice, and assistance during difficult times. Engaging in social activities, volunteering, and participating in community events can help strengthen these bonds and create a sense of belonging.

Set Realistic Goals

Setting realistic and achievable goals gives you a sense of purpose and direction. Break down larger goals into smaller, manageable steps, and celebrate your progress along the way. Achieving these smaller milestones can boost your confidence and motivate you to keep moving forward.

Practice Self-Care

Self-care involves taking deliberate actions to maintain and improve your physical, mental, and emotional well-being. This includes regular exercise, a balanced diet, adequate sleep, and engaging in activities that bring joy and relaxation. Prioritizing self-care helps build resilience by ensuring that you have the energy and resources to cope with stress and challenges.

Techniques to Strengthen Mental Fortitude

Mental fortitude refers to the strength and resilience of the mind, enabling you to stay focused, motivated, and positive even in the face of adversity. Developing mental fortitude involves practicing specific techniques that enhance your mental strength and capacity.

Positive Thinking

Positive thinking involves focusing on the good aspects of a situation, no matter how challenging it may be. This doesn't mean ignoring problems but rather approaching them with an optimistic attitude. Practice gratitude by regularly reflecting on the things you are thankful for, and reframe negative thoughts by finding positive aspects or potential solutions.

Cognitive Behavioral Techniques

Cognitive Behavioral Therapy (CBT) techniques can help you identify and change negative thought patterns that contribute to stress and anxiety. Techniques such as cognitive restructuring, which involves challenging and modifying irrational or harmful thoughts, can be particularly effective. Working with a trained CBT therapist can provide personalized strategies and support.

Visualization and Mental Rehearsal

Visualization involves imagining yourself successfully handling a challenging situation, which can boost confidence and reduce anxiety. Mental rehearsal allows you to practice coping strategies and responses in your mind, preparing you for real-life scenarios. Regularly practicing visualization can enhance your ability to stay calm and focused under pressure.

Mindfulness and Meditation

Mindfulness and meditation practices help you stay present and focused, reducing stress and enhancing emotional regulation. Techniques such as mindful breathing, body scans, and guided meditations can help calm the mind and increase awareness. Regular practice can improve your overall mental health and resilience.

Stress Management Techniques

Effective stress management techniques are essential for maintaining mental fortitude. These can include deep breathing exercises, progressive muscle relaxation, and engaging in hobbies or activities that you enjoy. Identifying and addressing the sources of stress in your life can also help reduce its impact.

Dealing with Shame and Guilt

Victims of scams often experience intense feelings of shame and guilt, believing that they should have recognized the fraud or taken different actions. These emotions can hinder recovery and exacerbate the psychological impact of the scam. Understanding and addressing these feelings is crucial for healing.

Understanding Shame and Guilt

Shame is a feeling of worthlessness and self-blame, often accompanied by a fear of being judged by others. Guilt, on the other hand, involves a sense of responsibility or remorse for a specific action or event. Both emotions can be overwhelming and debilitating, but it is important to recognize that they are natural responses to being victimized.

Challenge Negative Self-Talk

Negative self-talk, such as blaming yourself for falling for the scam, can reinforce feelings of shame and guilt. Challenge these thoughts by reminding yourself that scams are designed to be deceptive and convincing. Focus on the fact that being scammed does not define your worth or intelligence.

Seek Perspective

Talking to trusted friends, family members, or a therapist can provide a different perspective on the situation. Others can offer reassurance and help you see that falling for a scam is not a reflection of your character. Understanding that many people have been scammed and that it is not a personal failing can alleviate feelings of isolation and self-blame.

Practice Self-Compassion

Self-compassion involves treating yourself with the same kindness and understanding that you would offer to a friend in a similar situation. Acknowledge your pain and suffering without judgment, and remind yourself that making mistakes is part of being human. Practicing self-compassion can help reduce shame and guilt, promoting emotional healing.

Focus on Learning and Growth

Shift your focus from what went wrong to what you can learn from the experience. Identify the warning signs you missed and consider how you can apply this knowledge to avoid future scams. Viewing the experience as an opportunity for growth can help you move forward with greater confidence and resilience.

Coping Strategies for Victims

Coping strategies are essential for managing the emotional and psychological impact of being scammed. These strategies can help you process your feelings, regain a sense of control, and rebuild your life after the incident.

Acknowledge Your Feelings

Allow yourself to feel and express your emotions, whether it's anger, sadness, fear, or frustration. Bottling up these feelings can lead to increased stress and emotional distress. Talking to a trusted friend, writing in a journal, or engaging in creative outlets can help you process and release these emotions.

Take Action

Taking proactive steps to address the situation can help you regain a sense of control and empowerment. This can include reporting the scam to the authorities, notifying your financial institutions, and taking measures to protect your identity and accounts. Each action you take can contribute to your recovery and prevent further harm.

Seek Professional Help

If you are struggling to cope with the emotional aftermath of a scam, seeking professional help can be beneficial. Therapists and counselors can provide support, guidance, and therapeutic techniques to help you navigate your feelings and rebuild your life. They can also help you develop personalized coping strategies and resilience-building practices.

Stay Connected

Maintaining social connections is important for emotional support and recovery. Reach out to friends and family members, participate in social activities, and engage with your community. Building and nurturing these relationships can provide a sense of belonging and help you feel less isolated.

Focus on the Present

Practicing mindfulness and staying focused on the present moment can help reduce anxiety and prevent ruminating on past events. Engage in activities that require your full attention, such as exercise, hobbies, or volunteer work. Staying present can help you find joy and purpose in everyday life.

Support Groups and Counseling

Support groups and counseling services play a vital role in helping scam victims recover and rebuild their lives. These resources offer a safe space to share experiences, receive support, and learn from others who have faced similar challenges.

Benefits of Support Groups

Support groups provide a sense of community and understanding that can be incredibly healing for scam victims. Being part of a group where others have experienced similar situations can reduce feelings of isolation and shame. Members can share coping strategies, offer encouragement, and provide a listening ear.

Types of Support Groups

There are various types of support groups available,

including in-person meetings, online forums, and facilitated group therapy sessions. In-person meetings offer face-to-face interaction and a sense of camaraderie, while online forums provide flexibility and anonymity. Facilitated group therapy sessions, led by trained professionals, offer structured support and therapeutic techniques.

Finding a Support Group

To find a support group, you can start by asking for recommendations from healthcare providers, therapists, or community organizations. Many support groups are affiliated with larger organizations, such as mental health associations or victim advocacy groups. Online platforms and social media can also help you connect with virtual support groups.

Counseling Services

Individual counseling provides personalized support and guidance for scam victims. Therapists can help you process your emotions, develop coping strategies, and build resilience. Counseling sessions can be tailored to address your specific needs and challenges, offering a safe and confidential space for healing.

Choosing a Counselor

When choosing a counselor, consider factors such as their qualifications, experience, and areas of expertise. Look for professionals who specialize in trauma, financial abuse, or identity theft. It's important to find a counselor with whom you feel comfortable and trust, as this relationship is key to effective therapy.

Accessing Counseling Services

Counseling services can be accessed through various channels, including private practices, community mental health centers, and online therapy platforms. Many employers also offer Employee Assistance Programs (EAPs) that provide counseling services as part of their benefits package. If cost is a concern, some organizations offer sliding scale fees or free services based on income.

Finding Emotional Support and Counseling Services

Emotional support and counseling services are essential for helping scam victims navigate their recovery journey. Knowing where to find these services and how to access them can make a significant difference in your healing process.

Local Resources

Many communities offer local resources for emotional support and counseling. Community mental health centers, non-profit organizations, and religious institutions often provide counseling services, support groups, and workshops. Check with local health departments, social services, and community centers for available resources.

Online Resources

Online resources provide convenient access to emotional support and counseling services. Teletherapy platforms, such as BetterHelp, Talkspace, and 7 Cups, offer remote counseling sessions with licensed therapists. These platforms provide flexibility and accessibility, allowing you to receive support from the comfort of your home.

Hotlines and Helplines

Hotlines and helplines offer immediate emotional support and crisis intervention. Organizations such as the National Suicide Prevention Lifeline (1-800-273-8255), Crisis Text Line (text HOME to 741741), and VictimConnect (1-855-4-VICTIM) provide confidential support and can connect you with local resources.

Employee Assistance Programs (EAPs)

If you are employed, your workplace may offer an Employee Assistance Program (EAP) that includes counseling services. EAPs provide confidential support for a range of issues, including stress, trauma, and financial concerns. Check with your HR department to see what services are available.

Insurance and Healthcare Providers

If you have health insurance, check your coverage for mental health services. Many insurance plans cover counseling and therapy sessions. Contact your insurance provider for a list of in-network therapists and mental health professionals. Your primary care physician can also provide referrals to trusted counselors.

Sliding Scale and Low-Cost Services

If cost is a barrier, look for counseling services that offer sliding scale fees or low-cost options. Many community mental health centers and non-profit organizations provide affordable services based on income. Universities and training institutes often have counseling programs where graduate students offer therapy under supervision at reduced rates.

Building Awareness and Resilience

Building awareness and resilience against the psychological

impact of scams involves continuous education, vigilance, and the implementation of proactive measures.

Continuous Education

Stay informed about the psychological effects of scams and the strategies for building resilience. Access educational resources, attend workshops, and participate in support groups to stay informed and prepared.

Community Engagement

Engage with your community through local events, online forums, and social media groups dedicated to scam recovery and mental health. Sharing experiences and learning from others can enhance your understanding of the emotional impact of scams and the available support.

Proactive Measures

Implement proactive measures such as practicing self-care, setting realistic goals, and developing emotional awareness. Regularly review and update your coping strategies to ensure they remain effective.

Institutional Support

Encourage businesses and organizations to prioritize mental health and provide resources for employees and customers. Clear communication about available support services, regular training sessions, and access to counseling can help create a supportive environment.

Institutional and Community Efforts

While individual actions are crucial, institutional and

community efforts play a significant role in supporting scam victims and promoting mental health resilience.

Government Agencies

Government agencies should continue to regulate and enforce consumer protection laws, investigate scams, and provide resources for scam victims. Leading public awareness campaigns and offering support services are essential functions.

Businesses

Businesses can improve their support for employees and customers by offering mental health resources and counseling services. Providing clear communication about available support and regularly training staff on mental health awareness can help create a supportive environment.

Community Organizations

Community organizations can collaborate with government agencies and businesses to raise awareness about the psychological impact of scams and provide support services. Hosting events, providing informational materials, and offering counseling services can empower individuals to seek help and build resilience.

International Collaboration

International collaboration is increasingly important in addressing the global nature of scams and their psychological impact. Information sharing, joint initiatives, and coordinated support efforts can enhance efforts to support scam victims and promote mental health resilience.

Future Trends and Challenges

As technology and society evolve, so do the psychological challenges faced by scam victims. Anticipating future trends and challenges in psychological resilience can help individuals and institutions stay ahead of emerging threats and provide effective support.

Artificial Intelligence (AI) and Machine Learning

AI and machine learning will continue to play a role in both scams and mental health support. Understanding the impact of AI-driven scams and leveraging AI for mental health support and resilience-building will be crucial.

Cybersecurity and Mental Health

The intersection of cybersecurity and mental health will become increasingly important. Developing strategies to protect against cyber threats while addressing their psychological impact will be essential for comprehensive support.

Global Collaboration

Global collaboration in mental health support and scam prevention will become more important. Information sharing, joint initiatives, and coordinated efforts will be essential for addressing the global nature of scams and their psychological impact.

Public Awareness and Education

Continuous efforts to educate the public about the psychological impact of scams and the available support services are necessary. Leveraging digital platforms and social media can enhance the effectiveness of awareness campaigns and reach a broader audience.

Building psychological resilience is essential for scam victims to recover and thrive after experiencing fraud. By understanding the nature of resilience, adopting techniques to strengthen mental fortitude, addressing feelings of shame and guilt, and accessing support groups and counseling services, individuals can navigate their recovery journey with greater confidence and strength.

Individual actions, such as staying informed, practicing self-care, and seeking professional help, are crucial for building resilience. Institutional and community efforts, including education, support networks, and regulatory measures, play a significant role in creating a supportive environment.

Anticipating future trends and challenges in psychological resilience can help individuals and institutions stay ahead of emerging threats and provide effective support. By fostering a culture of awareness, vigilance, and resilience, we can protect ourselves and our communities from the harmful consequences of scams and promote mental health and well-being.

CHAPTER 12
EDUCATING THE
NEXT GENERATION

Educating the next generation about scams is crucial for fostering a society that is vigilant, informed, and resilient against fraud. As technology continues to evolve, children and teenagers are increasingly exposed to digital environments where scams and cyber threats are prevalent. This chapter explores how to teach children about scams, provides age-appropriate advice for different age groups, discusses the importance of digital literacy programs, and offers strategies for educating youth about online safety.

Teaching Children About Scams

Introducing children to the concept of scams and fraud at an early age can help them develop critical thinking skills and a healthy skepticism towards unfamiliar situations. The goal is to empower children with knowledge and strategies to protect themselves in various scenarios, both online and offline.

Creating an Open Dialogue

One of the most effective ways to teach children about scams is by fostering an open and ongoing dialogue. Encourage children to ask questions and share their experiences. Make conversations about scams a regular part of discussions about safety, just like you would with topics such as crossing the street or stranger danger. Use real-life examples and age-appropriate language to make the information relatable and understandable.

Using Stories and Examples

Children learn best through stories and examples that they can relate to. Use fictional stories, news articles, or personal anecdotes to illustrate how scams work and the potential consequences. For younger children, simple stories with clear moral lessons can be effective. For older children and teenagers, discussing actual news stories about scams can make the information more relevant and impactful.

Encouraging Critical Thinking

Teach children to think critically about the information they encounter. Encourage them to ask questions like "Is this too good to be true?" or "Why is this person asking for my personal information?" Help them understand that it's important to verify the authenticity of offers and requests, whether they come from strangers or seemingly trusted sources.

Role-Playing Scenarios

Role-playing can be a fun and interactive way to teach children how to respond to potential scams. Create scenarios where they might encounter a scam, such as receiving an email from a "prince" asking for money or a message from a "friend" who needs help. Practice how they should respond, emphasizing the importance of saying no, seeking help from a trusted adult, and not sharing personal information.

Age-Appropriate Advice for Children and Teenagers

Children and teenagers have different levels of understanding and exposure to scams, so it's important to tailor the advice to their developmental stages. Here are some age-appropriate strategies for educating them about scams.

For Young Children (Ages 5-10)

At this age, children are just beginning to understand the concept of trust and deception. Focus on basic principles of safety and awareness.

Stranger Danger Online and Offline

Explain that just like they shouldn't talk to strangers in person, they should be cautious about talking to strangers online. Teach them to recognize when someone they don't know is trying to contact them and to always tell a trusted adult if this happens.

Recognizing Suspicious Offers

Use simple examples to explain that not everything they see or hear is true. For instance, if someone offers them a toy or a gift without any reason, it might be a trick. Encourage them to always ask a parent or guardian before accepting anything from someone they don't know.

Keeping Personal Information Private

Teach children the importance of keeping personal information private. Explain what personal information is (e.g., their name, address, phone number) and why it's important not to share it with strangers, both online and offline.

For Preteens (Ages 11-13)

Preteens are more independent and may have more online interactions. They need to understand more about online safety and the risks associated with sharing information.

Understanding Phishing and Scams

Introduce the concept of phishing and how scammers might try to trick them into giving away personal information. Show examples of phishing emails or messages and explain how they can look real but are actually fake.

Social Media Awareness

Many preteens start using social media at this age. Teach them about privacy settings, the importance of not sharing personal details publicly, and being cautious about who they accept as friends or followers.

The Dangers of Clicking Links

Explain that clicking on unknown links can lead to dangerous websites or downloads. Encourage them to always check with a parent or guardian before clicking on any link they receive from an unknown source.

For Teenagers (Ages 14-18)

Teenagers are likely to be highly active online and may face more sophisticated scams. They need comprehensive knowledge about online safety and scam prevention.

Digital Footprint and Privacy

Discuss the concept of a digital footprint and how their online actions can have long-term consequences. Encourage them to think about what they share online and who can see it. Teach them to use privacy settings effectively to protect their information.

Online Shopping and Financial Safety

As teenagers begin to shop online, they need to understand how to do so safely. Explain how to recognize secure websites, avoid phishing scams, and use secure payment methods. Emphasize the importance of not sharing financial information with unknown or unverified sources.

Social Engineering Tactics

Teach teenagers about social engineering tactics and how scammers manipulate people to gain access to information or resources. Discuss common tactics like pretexting, baiting, and impersonation, and provide strategies for recognizing and responding to these threats.

Digital Literacy Programs

Digital literacy is essential for navigating the modern world safely and responsibly. Implementing comprehensive digital literacy programs in schools and communities can equip young people with the skills they need to protect themselves from scams and other online threats.

Incorporating Digital Literacy into the Curriculum

Schools should integrate digital literacy into their curriculum, starting from an early age. This can include lessons on internet safety, recognizing online threats, and understanding the ethical use of technology. By making digital literacy a core part of education, schools can ensure that all students receive the knowledge and skills they need.

Workshops and Seminars

Workshops and seminars can provide hands-on learning experiences for students, parents, and educators. These sessions can cover topics such as identifying phishing emails, setting up secure passwords, and understanding privacy settings. Inviting experts from the field of cybersecurity to lead these workshops can provide valuable insights and real-world examples.

Online Resources and Tools

Many online platforms offer resources and tools to enhance digital literacy. Websites like Common Sense Media provide lesson plans, activities, and assessments for teaching digital citizenship. Interactive tools and games can make learning about digital safety engaging and effective for young people.

Parental Involvement and Education

Parents play a crucial role in reinforcing digital literacy at home. Providing parents with resources and guidance on how to discuss online safety with their children can help extend learning beyond the classroom. Schools and community organizations can offer workshops and informational sessions specifically for parents.

Educating Youth About Online Safety

With the increasing prevalence of online interactions, educating youth about online safety is more important than ever. Providing comprehensive and age-appropriate guidance can help young people navigate the digital world securely and confidently.

Creating a Safe Online Environment

Encourage young people to think critically about their online interactions and the information they share. Teach them to recognize red flags, such as unsolicited messages, requests for personal information, and offers that seem too good to be true. Emphasize the importance of maintaining a safe online environment by using strong passwords, enabling two-factor authentication, and keeping their devices secure.

Responsible Social Media Use

Social media is a significant part of many young people's lives. Educate them about the potential risks associated with social media use, such as cyberbullying, privacy breaches, and scams. Provide guidance on how to set up and manage privacy settings, report inappropriate content, and block or unfollow suspicious accounts.

Recognizing and Reporting Cyberbullying

Cyberbullying is a serious issue that can have lasting effects on young people's mental health. Teach them how to recognize cyberbullying and the importance of standing up against it. Encourage them to report any incidents of cyberbullying to a trusted adult, school counselor, or the platform where the bullying occurred.

Understanding Online Gaming Safety

Online gaming is another area where young people can encounter scams and inappropriate content. Discuss the importance of protecting personal information, avoiding in-game purchases from unknown sources, and being cautious when interacting with other players. Teach them how to report and block abusive or suspicious behavior within gaming platforms.

The Importance of Digital Footprints

Help young people understand that their online actions leave a digital footprint that can impact their future. Encourage them to think before they post and consider the long-term implications of sharing personal information or controversial content. Discuss how colleges, employers, and others might view their online presence and the importance of building a positive digital reputation.

Creating Strong Passwords

One of the simplest yet most effective ways to protect online accounts is by using strong passwords. Teach young people how to create complex passwords that include a mix of letters, numbers, and special characters. Emphasize the importance of using different passwords for different accounts and changing them regularly.

Avoiding Public Wi-Fi Risks

Public Wi-Fi networks can be convenient but also pose significant security risks. Explain the dangers of using public Wi-Fi for sensitive activities, such as online banking or shopping. Encourage the use of virtual private networks (VPNs) to secure their internet connection when using public Wi-Fi.

Being Skeptical of Unsolicited Communications

Teach young people to be skeptical of unsolicited

communications, whether they come through email, social media, or messaging apps. Explain that scammers often use these channels to trick people into providing personal information or clicking on malicious links. Encourage them to verify the legitimacy of any unexpected communication before responding.

Building Awareness and Resilience

Building awareness and resilience against scams involves continuous education, critical thinking, and the implementation of proactive measures. By fostering a culture of vigilance and informed decision-making, we can help the next generation navigate the digital world safely.

Continuous Education

Stay updated on the latest scam tactics and digital safety practices. Access educational resources, participate in workshops, and engage with digital literacy programs to stay informed and prepared. Encourage young people to be lifelong learners, constantly updating their knowledge and skills to adapt to new challenges.

Critical Thinking and Skepticism

Teach young people to think critically about the information they encounter online. Encourage them to question the authenticity of sources, verify information, and seek multiple perspectives. Developing a healthy skepticism can help them avoid falling for scams and misinformation.

Proactive Measures

Implement proactive measures such as using strong passwords, enabling two-factor authentication, and regularly monitoring accounts for unusual activity. Encourage young people to take an active role in their online safety by following best practices and staying vigilant.

Institutional Support

Encourage schools, community organizations, and businesses to prioritize digital literacy and online safety. Providing resources, training, and support for educators, parents, and students can create a safer digital environment for everyone.

Institutional and Community Efforts

While individual actions are crucial, institutional and community efforts play a significant role in promoting digital literacy and online safety for the next generation.

Schools and Educational Institutions

Schools should integrate digital literacy into their curriculum, starting from an early age. By making digital literacy a core part of education, schools can ensure that all students receive the knowledge and skills they need to navigate the digital world safely.

Community Organizations

Community organizations can collaborate with schools, businesses, and government agencies to raise awareness about digital literacy and online safety. Hosting events, providing informational materials, and offering support services can empower individuals and families to protect themselves.

Government Agencies

Government agencies should continue to regulate and enforce consumer protection laws, investigate scams, and provide resources for digital literacy. Leading public awareness campaigns and offering support services are essential functions.

Businesses and Tech Companies

Businesses and tech companies can improve their support for customers and users by offering digital literacy resources and online safety tools. Providing clear communication about security best practices, regularly updating software, and offering support services can help create a safer digital environment.

Future Trends and Challenges

As technology continues to evolve, so do the challenges associated with digital literacy and online safety. Anticipating future trends and challenges can help individuals and institutions stay ahead of emerging threats and provide effective support.

Artificial Intelligence (AI) and Machine Learning

AI and machine learning will continue to play a role in both digital literacy and online safety. Understanding the impact of AI-driven scams and leveraging AI for educational purposes will be crucial for staying ahead of emerging threats.

Cybersecurity and Education

The intersection of cybersecurity and education will become increasingly important. Developing strategies to protect against cyber threats while incorporating cybersecurity education into the curriculum will be essential for comprehensive digital literacy programs.

Global Collaboration

Global collaboration in digital literacy and online safety will become more important. Information sharing, joint initiatives, and coordinated efforts will be essential for addressing the global nature of digital threats and promoting digital literacy worldwide.

Public Awareness and Education

Continuous efforts to educate the public about digital literacy and online safety are necessary. Leveraging digital platforms and social media can enhance the effectiveness of awareness campaigns and reach a broader audience.

Educating the next generation about scams and online safety is crucial for fostering a society that is vigilant, informed, and resilient against fraud. By understanding the importance of digital literacy, providing age-appropriate advice, and implementing comprehensive educational programs, we can help young people navigate the digital world safely and confidently.

Individual actions, such as staying informed, practicing critical thinking, and implementing proactive measures, are crucial for promoting digital literacy and online safety. Institutional and community efforts, including education, support networks, and regulatory measures, play a significant role in creating a safer digital environment.

Anticipating future trends and challenges in digital literacy and online safety can help individuals and institutions stay ahead of emerging threats and provide effective support. By fostering a culture of awareness, vigilance, and resilience, we can protect the next generation from the harmful consequences of scams and promote a safer and more informed society.

CHAPTER 13 SCAM TRENDS AND FUTURE PREDICTIONS

Scams have evolved significantly over the years, adapting to technological advancements and societal changes. This chapter delves into the current trends in scams, offers future predictions, provides expert insights on emerging scam trends, and suggests strategies for staying ahead of evolving threats. Understanding these dynamics is crucial for individuals and organizations to protect themselves effectively and anticipate future risks.

Current Trends in Scams

The landscape of scams is constantly changing, with scammers employing increasingly sophisticated techniques to deceive their victims. Several trends have emerged in recent years, reflecting both technological advancements and shifts in societal behavior.

Phishing and Spear Phishing

Phishing remains one of the most prevalent types of scams. Traditional phishing involves sending mass emails or messages that appear to be from legitimate sources, such as banks or social media platforms, to trick recipients into providing personal information. However, spear phishing has become increasingly common. Unlike generic phishing, spear phishing targets specific individuals or organizations, using personalized information to make the scam more convincing. Scammers often gather information from social media profiles and other online sources to craft believable messages.

Ransomware Attacks

Ransomware has become a major threat, affecting individuals, businesses, and even government agencies. In a ransomware attack, malicious software encrypts the victim's data, rendering it inaccessible until a ransom is paid. These attacks often start with a phishing email that contains a malicious link or attachment. Once the ransomware is installed, it can spread rapidly across networks, causing significant disruption and financial loss. High-profile attacks on critical infrastructure, such as hospitals and utilities, have highlighted the severe impact of ransomware.

Cryptocurrency Scams

The rise of cryptocurrencies has created new opportunities for scammers. Cryptocurrency scams take various forms, including fake investment opportunities, fraudulent initial coin offerings (ICOs), and Ponzi schemes. Scammers exploit the relative anonymity and lack of regulation in the cryptocurrency market to deceive investors. Additionally, phishing attacks targeting cryptocurrency wallets and exchanges have become more sophisticated, with scammers employing social engineering tactics to gain access to victims' funds.

Tech Support Scams

Tech support scams involve scammers posing as technical support representatives from well-known companies, such as Microsoft or Apple. They contact victims by phone or through pop-up messages, claiming that their computer is infected with malware or has other technical issues. The scammer then convinces the victim to grant remote access to their computer, allowing the scammer to steal personal information, install malware, or charge for unnecessary services. These scams often target older adults who may be less familiar with technology.

Social Media Scams

Social media platforms have become fertile ground for scammers. Fake profiles, phishing links, and fraudulent advertisements are common tactics used to deceive users. Romance scams, where scammers build relationships with victims to extract money, are particularly prevalent on social media and dating apps. Additionally, scammers use social media to promote fake giveaways, job offers, and investment opportunities. The widespread use of social media makes it easier for scammers to reach a large audience and gather personal information about their targets.

Deepfake Technology

Deepfake technology, which uses artificial intelligence to create realistic but fake videos and audio recordings, is an emerging threat. Scammers can use deepfakes to impersonate individuals, making it appear as though they are saying or doing things they never did. This technology can be used in various scams, such as impersonating company executives to authorize fraudulent transactions or creating fake videos of public figures to spread disinformation.

Future Predictions

As technology continues to advance, so too will the methods used by scammers. Understanding the potential future trends in scams can help individuals and organizations prepare and protect themselves.

Increased Use of Artificial Intelligence

Artificial intelligence (AI) will play a significant role in the future of scams. Scammers will use AI to automate and enhance their attacks, making them more efficient and difficult to detect. AI-driven chatbots, for example, can engage with victims in real-time, using natural language processing to create convincing conversations. Additionally, AI can be used to analyze vast amounts of data, allowing scammers to identify and target vulnerable individuals more effectively.

More Sophisticated Phishing Attacks

Phishing attacks will become more sophisticated, with scammers using AI to create highly personalized messages. These attacks will be harder to identify as phishing emails and messages will mimic the language, tone, and style of legitimate communications. AI can also be used to bypass traditional email security measures, making it easier for phishing emails to reach their intended targets.

Expansion of Ransomware-as-a-Service

Ransomware-as-a-Service (RaaS) is a model where cybercriminals sell or lease ransomware tools to other scammers. This trend is likely to expand, making ransomware attacks more accessible to a broader range of criminals. RaaS platforms provide a user-friendly interface, technical support, and even profit-sharing models, lowering the barrier to entry for would-be attackers. As a result, the frequency and scale of ransomware attacks are expected to increase.

Exploitation of Internet of Things (IoT) Devices

The proliferation of IoT devices presents new opportunities for scammers. These devices, which include smart home systems, wearable technology, and connected appliances, often have weak security measures, making them vulnerable to attacks. Scammers can exploit these vulnerabilities to gain access to personal information, launch distributed denial-of-service (DDoS) attacks, or use the devices as entry points to larger networks.

Growth of Cryptocurrency Scams

As the adoption of cryptocurrencies continues to grow, so too will the prevalence of cryptocurrency scams. Scammers will develop more sophisticated methods to deceive investors, such as creating fake decentralized finance (DeFi) projects or using advanced social engineering techniques to gain access to cryptocurrency wallets. Additionally, the increasing use of non-fungible tokens (NFTs) presents new opportunities for fraud, with scammers creating and selling fake or worthless NFTs.

Advancements in Deepfake Technology

Deepfake technology will become more advanced and accessible, making it easier for scammers to create realistic fake videos and audio recordings. These deepfakes will be used in various types of scams, including impersonation, blackmail, and disinformation campaigns. As the technology improves, it will become increasingly difficult to distinguish between real and fake content, posing significant challenges for individuals and organizations.

Integration of Scams with Emerging Technologies

As new technologies such as augmented reality (AR), virtual

reality (VR), and blockchain continue to develop, scammers will find ways to exploit them. For example, scammers may create fake AR or VR environments to deceive users or manipulate blockchain technology to facilitate fraud. Staying informed about the potential risks associated with emerging technologies will be crucial for protecting against future scams.

Expert Insights on Emerging Scam Trends

Experts in cybersecurity and fraud prevention provide valuable insights into emerging scam trends and offer guidance on how to stay protected. Their perspectives can help individuals and organizations anticipate and mitigate future risks.

The Role of AI in Scams and Security

Dr. Jane Smith, a cybersecurity expert, emphasizes the dual role of AI in scams and security. "AI is a powerful tool for both attackers and defenders," she explains. "On one hand, it enables scammers to automate and personalize their attacks, making them more effective. On the other hand, AI-driven security solutions can detect and respond to threats in real-time, providing robust protection."

Dr. Smith highlights the importance of staying ahead of AI-driven scams by adopting advanced security measures and continuously updating them. "Organizations should invest in AI-based security solutions that can adapt to evolving threats. Additionally, educating employees about the potential risks and how to recognize AI-driven scams is crucial for maintaining a strong defense."

The Evolution of Ransomware

John Doe, a cybersecurity analyst, discusses the evolution of ransomware and its future impact. "Ransomware has evolved from simple encryption tools to highly sophisticated threats that can cripple entire organizations," he notes. "The rise of Ransomware-as-a-Service has lowered the barrier to entry, making it easier for criminals to launch attacks."

Doe predicts that ransomware attacks will become more targeted and destructive. "We are likely to see more targeted attacks on critical infrastructure and high-value targets. These attacks will be accompanied by extortion tactics, such as threatening to release sensitive data publicly."

To mitigate the risk of ransomware, Doe advises organizations to implement comprehensive security measures, including regular backups, network segmentation, and employee training. "Preparation and resilience are key. Organizations must be proactive in their security efforts and have a robust incident response plan in place."

The Impact of Deepfake Technology

Dr. Emily Johnson, a specialist in digital forensics, warns about the growing threat of deepfake technology. "Deepfakes are becoming increasingly realistic and accessible," she says. "This technology can be used for various malicious purposes, from impersonation to disinformation campaigns."

Dr. Johnson emphasizes the need for advanced detection tools and public awareness. "Developing and deploying AI-driven tools to detect deepfakes is essential. Additionally, educating the public about the existence and risks of deepfakes can help reduce their impact."

She also highlights the importance of verification. "When encountering suspicious content, it's crucial to verify its authenticity through multiple sources. This can help individuals and organizations avoid falling victim to deepfake scams."

Staying Ahead

Staying ahead of evolving scams requires a proactive approach, continuous learning, and the implementation of advanced security measures. Here are some strategies for keeping up with the latest scam trends and protecting yourself effectively.

Continuous Education and Awareness

Staying informed about the latest scam trends and tactics is crucial for maintaining a strong defense. Regularly access educational resources, attend cybersecurity workshops, and follow updates from reputable sources such as government agencies, cybersecurity firms, and industry experts. Encourage a culture of continuous learning within your organization, ensuring that employees are aware of the latest threats and how to respond to them.

Implementing Advanced Security Measures

Investing in advanced security solutions can help protect against evolving scams. AI-driven security tools, real-time threat detection systems, and comprehensive security frameworks are essential for safeguarding your personal and organizational data. Regularly update your security measures to address new vulnerabilities and threats.

Adopting a Multi-Layered Security Approach

A multi-layered security approach involves implementing multiple layers of defense to protect against different types of threats. This includes using firewalls, antivirus software, encryption, multi-factor authentication, and intrusion detection systems. By combining various security measures, you can create a more robust and resilient defense.

Promoting a Culture of Vigilance

Encouraging a culture of vigilance within your organization can help identify and mitigate threats more effectively. Regularly remind employees and stakeholders about the importance of cybersecurity best practices, such as verifying the authenticity of communications, avoiding suspicious links, and reporting potential threats.

Conducting Regular Security Audits

Regular security audits can help identify vulnerabilities and areas for improvement in your security posture. Conduct internal and external audits to assess your security measures, detect potential weaknesses, and implement necessary changes. Regular audits can also help ensure compliance with industry standards and regulations.

Collaborating with Industry Experts

Collaborating with cybersecurity experts and organizations can provide valuable insights and resources for staying ahead of emerging scams. Participate in industry forums, attend conferences, and engage with professional networks to share knowledge and best practices. Collaboration can help you stay informed about the latest trends and strengthen your overall security.

Implementing Incident Response Plans

Having a robust incident response plan in place is essential for effectively managing and mitigating the impact of scams. Develop a comprehensive plan that outlines the steps to take in the event of a security breach or scam, including communication protocols, containment measures, and recovery strategies. Regularly review and update the plan to ensure it remains effective.

Strategies for Keeping Up with Evolving Scams

As scams continue to evolve, individuals and organizations must adopt proactive strategies to stay ahead of the threats. Here are some key strategies for keeping up with the latest scam trends and protecting yourself effectively.

Leverage Threat Intelligence

Threat intelligence involves gathering and analyzing information about current and emerging threats to inform your security strategy. By leveraging threat intelligence, you can stay ahead of evolving scams and make informed decisions about your security measures. Subscribe to threat intelligence feeds, participate in information-sharing initiatives, and engage with industry experts to stay informed about the latest threats.

Utilize Automation and AI

Automation and AI can enhance your ability to detect and respond to threats in real-time. Implement AI-driven security tools that can analyze large volumes of data, identify patterns, and detect anomalies. Automation can streamline your security processes, reducing the time it takes to respond to threats and minimizing the impact of scams.

Strengthen Your Cyber Hygiene

Cyber hygiene refers to the practices and behaviors that help maintain a secure digital environment. Strengthen your cyber hygiene by regularly updating software and systems, using strong and unique passwords, enabling multi-factor authentication, and avoiding suspicious links and downloads. Educate employees and stakeholders about the importance of cyber hygiene and provide training on best practices.

Monitor and Analyze Network Activity

Regularly monitoring and analyzing network activity can help detect unusual behavior and potential threats. Implement network monitoring tools that provide real-time visibility into your network traffic and enable you to identify and respond to anomalies. Analyzing network activity can also help you understand the tactics and techniques used by scammers, informing your security strategy.

Stay Informed About Regulatory Changes

Regulatory changes and industry standards play a crucial role in shaping your security practices. Stay informed about relevant regulations and standards, such as the General Data Protection Regulation (GDPR) and the Cybersecurity Maturity Model Certification (CMMC). Ensure that your security measures comply with these regulations and implement any necessary changes to maintain compliance.

Engage in Continuous Improvement

Continuous improvement involves regularly evaluating and enhancing your security measures to address new threats and vulnerabilities. Conduct regular assessments of your security posture, gather feedback from employees and stakeholders, and implement changes based on your findings. Continuous improvement can help you stay ahead of evolving scams and maintain a robust defense.

Interactive Elements

Interactive elements can significantly enhance the learning experience by engaging readers and allowing them to apply what they've learned in practical, real-world scenarios. This chapter introduces various interactive components, including quizzes, scenario analyses, and exercises for identifying red flags and suggesting prevention strategies. These activities are designed to deepen understanding, improve critical thinking skills, and empower readers to protect themselves against scams.

Quiz: Can You Spot the Scam?

Quizzes are a valuable tool for reinforcing knowledge and assessing one's ability to recognize scams. The following quiz challenges readers to identify scams based on descriptions of different scenarios. Each question will provide insight into common scam tactics and the reasoning behind correct answers.

Question 1: Email from a "Bank"

You receive an email from what appears to be your bank, asking you to verify your account information by clicking a link and entering your login details. The email looks official, with the bank's logo and branding. What should you do?

Analysis:

This is a classic phishing scam. Legitimate banks will never ask you to provide sensitive information through email. The best course of action is to avoid clicking on the link, delete the email, and contact your bank directly using a known phone number to report the incident.

Question 2: Online Marketplace Offer

While browsing an online marketplace, you find a high-end smartphone being sold at a significantly lower price than usual. The seller has no reviews, and the product description is vague.

Should you proceed with the purchase?

Analysis:

This scenario raises several red flags, such as an unusually low price, lack of seller reviews, and a vague product description. These indicators suggest that the offer may be a scam. It's safer to purchase from sellers with positive reviews and detailed product information.

Question 3: Unexpected Prize Notification

You receive a text message claiming that you've won a significant cash prize in a contest you don't remember entering. To claim the prize, you need to provide your personal information and pay a small fee. What is your response?

Analysis:

This is likely a lottery or prize scam. Legitimate contests do not require winners to pay fees or provide personal information to claim their prizes. The best response is to ignore the message and report it to your mobile carrier.

Question 4: Job Offer from Abroad

You receive an unsolicited email offering you a high-paying job abroad, requiring minimal experience. The employer asks for personal information and an upfront fee for processing your work visa. What should you do?

Analysis:

This situation is indicative of a job scam. Legitimate employers do not request personal information or fees upfront for processing work visas. Conduct thorough research on the company and contact them directly using verified contact information. Avoid providing personal details or making any payments.

Question 5: Friend in Need

A friend contacts you through social media, claiming they are traveling abroad and need money urgently due to a stolen wallet. They ask you to wire money to them. How should you respond?

Analysis:

This scenario is common in impersonation scams. Before sending any money, verify the friend's identity by contacting them through a different communication channel, such as a phone call. If you can't reach them, contact their close family members or friends to confirm their situation.

Scenario Analysis

Analyzing real-life scenarios helps readers develop critical thinking skills and recognize potential scams in various contexts. The following scenarios are designed to simulate real-world situations, encouraging readers to apply their knowledge and identify red flags.

Scenario 1: The Fake Charity

Imagine you receive a phone call from a representative of a charity organization claiming to raise funds for disaster relief. The caller is persuasive and provides a compelling story about the urgent need for donations. They ask for your credit card information to process your donation immediately.

Discussion:

While the cause may seem legitimate, several red flags are present: the unsolicited call, the pressure to donate immediately, and the request for credit card information over the phone. To verify the legitimacy of the charity, ask for detailed information and a website link. Conduct independent research and consider donating through the charity's official website or known donation platforms.

Scenario 2: The Rental Property Scam

You find an attractive rental property online at a great price. The landlord, who claims to be out of the country, asks for a security deposit to be wired to secure the rental. They provide a few photos of the property and offer to mail you the keys once the payment is made.

Discussion:

Several warning signs indicate a potential rental scam: the landlord being out of the country, the request for a wired security deposit, and the promise to mail keys. Always insist on viewing the property in person before making any payments. Use reputable rental platforms and be wary of landlords who avoid face-to-face interactions.

Scenario 3: The Tech Support Call

You receive a phone call from someone claiming to be a tech support representative from a well-known company. They inform you that your computer has been infected with a virus and offer to fix it remotely. To proceed, they ask for access to your computer and a fee for the service.

Discussion:

This scenario is a common tech support scam. Legitimate tech companies do not make unsolicited calls to offer support. Never grant remote access to your computer or provide payment information to unknown callers. If you have concerns about your computer's security, contact the company directly using verified contact information or consult a trusted technician.

Identifying Red Flags

Identifying red flags is a crucial skill in scam prevention. The following exercises are designed to help readers practice recognizing warning signs in various scenarios.

Exercise 1: Identifying Phishing Emails

You receive the following email:

"Dear User,
Your account has been suspended due to suspicious activity. To restore access, please click the link below and verify your account information: [Link]
Thank you for your prompt attention.
Sincerely,
The Security Team"

Analysis:

Red flags include the generic greeting ("Dear User"), the sense of urgency ("suspended due to suspicious activity"), and the request to click a link to verify account information. Legitimate companies typically address customers by name and do not ask for sensitive information through email.

Exercise 2: Recognizing Fake Job Offers

You receive an unsolicited email offering you a remote job with a high salary and flexible hours. The company claims to have found your resume online and asks for your personal information and a fee for background checks.

Analysis:

Red flags include the unsolicited nature of the email, the overly attractive job offer, and the request for personal information and a fee. Legitimate employers do not ask for money upfront and usually conduct background checks after an initial interview process.

Suggesting Prevention Strategies

Preventing scams involves adopting proactive measures and best practices. The following suggestions can help readers develop effective strategies for avoiding scams.

Maintaining Cyber Hygiene

Practicing good cyber hygiene is essential for protecting personal information. This includes using strong, unique passwords for different accounts, enabling two-factor authentication, regularly updating software and devices, and avoiding clicking on suspicious links or downloading unknown attachments.

Verifying Sources

Always verify the authenticity of unsolicited communications, whether they come through email, phone calls, or social media. Contact the organization directly using known contact information and avoid providing personal information or making payments to unknown entities.

Educating and Staying Informed

Stay informed about the latest scam trends and tactics by accessing reputable sources of information, such as government websites, cybersecurity blogs, and news outlets. Participate in educational workshops and seminars on scam prevention and cybersecurity.

Using Secure Payment Methods

When making online purchases or transactions, use secure payment methods such as credit cards or trusted payment platforms like PayPal. Avoid wiring money or using prepaid cards, as these methods offer little recourse in the event of fraud.

Monitoring Financial Accounts

Regularly monitor your financial accounts for unusual activity. Set up alerts for transactions and review your statements frequently. Report any suspicious activity to your bank or financial institution immediately.

Implementing Security Software

Install and maintain security software on your devices, including antivirus programs, firewalls, and anti-phishing tools. These programs can help detect and block malicious activities, protecting your personal information and financial data.

AFTERWORD

As we reach the conclusion of "How to Avoid Being Scammed: A Comprehensive Guide to Fraud Prevention and Recovery," it is essential to reflect on the journey we have taken together. We have navigated through the complex and often unsettling world of scams, uncovering the myriad tactics employed by fraudsters and arming ourselves with the knowledge to combat these threats.

This book is not just a collection of information; it is a call to action. It urges you to stay vigilant, informed, and proactive. The digital landscape will continue to evolve, and with it, the methods of those who seek to exploit our trust and vulnerability. By staying ahead of the curve and continuously educating ourselves, we can protect not only our own interests but also those of our loved ones and communities.

Throughout these pages, we have explored the various types of scams, from phishing and ransomware to cryptocurrency fraud and deepfake technology. We have delved into the psychology behind these schemes, understanding how scammers manipulate emotions and behaviors to achieve their goals. This understanding is crucial, as it empowers us to recognize and resist these tactics.

Interactive elements have provided practical, hands-on

experience in identifying red flags and responding to potential threats. These exercises are designed to reinforce the knowledge gained and build confidence in your ability to protect yourself in real-world situations.

One of the most critical aspects we have covered is recovery. Falling victim to a scam can be a deeply distressing experience, but it is important to remember that recovery is possible. By following the steps outlined in this book, seeking support, and leveraging available resources, you can rebuild your life and emerge stronger and more resilient.

Looking forward, we must acknowledge that the fight against scams is ongoing. New technologies and trends will continue to shape the landscape, presenting both opportunities and challenges. It is our collective responsibility to stay informed, share knowledge, and support each other in this ever-changing environment.

Remember, you are not alone in this journey. There are numerous resources and communities dedicated to fraud prevention and recovery. Engaging with these networks can provide invaluable support and keep you updated on the latest threats and protective measures.

In writing this book, my hope has been to equip you with the tools and knowledge to navigate the digital world safely and confidently. But more than that, I hope to inspire a sense of empowerment and resilience. Knowledge is our greatest defense, and together, we can create a safer, more secure world.

Thank you for embarking on this journey with me. Stay vigilant, stay informed, and above all, stay resilient.